D1269666

Twayne's United States Authors Series

Sylvia E. Bowman, *Editor*

INDIANA UNIVERSITY

Waldo Frank

WALDO FRANK

By PAUL J. CARTER
University of Colorado

Twayne Publishers, Inc. :: New York

Library of Congress Catalog Card Number: 67-24766

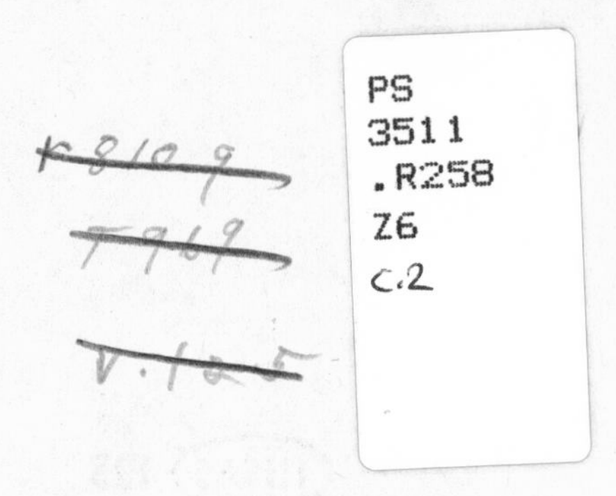

MANUFACTURED IN THE UNITED STATES OF AMERICA BY
UNITED PRINTING SERVICES, INC.
NEW HAVEN, CONN.

For

Jean Taylor Carter

Mary Moore Taylor

For

Jean Taylor Carter

Mary Moore Dutton

Preface

WALDO FRANK was a "man of letters" in the old sense of that phrase. For more than sixty years he devoted his energy, mind, and time to writing, with a single-minded dedication which produced fourteen novels, eighteen social histories, and over a hundred articles on literary and political subjects. Yet today Waldo Frank is known only vaguely by even literate and informed Americans; and most of his books are no longer in print, except in Latin America where he continues to be read and admired.[1]

One of the bright young men trying to help the United States come of age in the early 1920's, Frank became almost a celebrity as an editor of the stirring *Seven Arts* magazine and as the author of freshly experimental books translated into French, German, and Russian. In a short but highly laudatory study in 1923, Gorham Munson called Frank "the most exciting figure in contemporary American letters" and predicted that "as an artist in prose fiction he is likely to dominate the field in America for a time."[2] Thereafter Frank steadily lost his audience, although he wrote better novels and more significant cultural histories than those Munson praised. Today he is not even represented in the spawn of paperbacks, although as late as 1951 Charles Glicksberg admitted that Frank "is one of the few American critics who have achieved a truly international reputation."[3] But recent histories of criticism usually ignore him, and most of his critical essays remain hidden in the files of the magazines in which they first appeared.

Since Frank is one of the forgotten men of American letters, the best form for a description of his career would seem to be the presentation of a chronological narrative survey in which his writing is allowed to speak for itself and in which the emphasis is placed upon the nature and style of the individual work instead of a critical analysis of it. His books will have to be better known before critical dissection in the modern fashion is appropriate or useful; therefore, this commentary will simply try to prepare the way for some such future examination, as other studies of Frank's works have tried to do.

There are only three studies, one being Munson's early view. The other two are substantial books but of a limited nature since they are doctoral dissertations. William Bittner brilliantly analyzes the fiction in *The Novels of Waldo Frank* (1958), and

Jerome Kloucek characterizes with impressive skill and range the philosophical ideas and the literary heritage in *Waldo Frank: The Ground of His Mind and Art* (1963). My discussion is more deeply indebted to both of these excellent scholarly treatises than conventional acknowledgments will reveal; it leans heavily upon them for background and critical insights while letting Frank's prose speak for itself as much as possible.

Frank's career is a direct expression of his mystic faith in the unity of Being, or in organic wholeness, as he labels that unity. He derives his sense of wholeness from a complex amalgam of intuition and the ideas of Freud, Marx, and especially Spinoza, whose philosophy supplies the moral check for the ideological excesses of Freud and Marx. Frank projects his vision of oneness in his concept of the Person, a concept which identifies an individual transformed by his awareness of totality into a cosmically-oriented man. By purifying himself of egocentricity and selfishness, the Person achieves the mystic's unquestioning acceptance of life by finding love in all things. Frank's novels depict this process of the death of the self and the birth of the Person, and his cultural studies portray the influence of the Person in the social realm.

Frank's books are not puzzling if one remembers that the author's approach to literature, as well as to life, is intuitive and essentially religious without being theological or institutional. "The mystical experience is one of being," he writes; "the religious one of knowing." And he uses the word "God" only because there is no better one for identifying cosmic unity. However he rejects all anthropomorphic connotations of godhead and all egocentric projections of personality, such as a belief in an after-life or in cosmic concern for the fortunes of the individual.

Frank calls himself a "naturalistic mystic," because he considers the distinctive feature of his mysticism to be a strict correlation of knowing with acting, of living in the world instead of rejecting it in the fashion of Eastern mystics. He learned from the Hebrew prophets that "conviction without deed is bad ethics." The religion of the future, therefore, will be a product of methodology instead of theology; its objective will be to find ways of action, public as well as private, which will release awareness of God or of cosmic wholeness. "*Act* in a certain way," Frank observes in one of his notebooks, "and you will know God. Like happiness, and like beauty, conscience of God is an indirect result of certain kinds of human behavior."[4] Thus the artist works to realize God, and his work of art becomes a "proof" of God. This concept is what young Waldo Frank was fumbling to express when at the age of fourteen he scribbled in a copybook a declaration: "Each of my works shall be a proof of God."

Frank's career is an attempt to make man aware of his bond with the cosmos and at the same time to create a culture in which spiritual values can survive and flourish through art. He has tried to transform America, to shape organic wholeness out of the fragmentation and chaos of contemporary existence. He would achieve this modern synthesis by reviving in American intellectual and political life the values of what he calls "The Great Tradition," his term for the kind of spiritual unity inherent in the Judeo-Christian tradition which reached its highest and finest expression in the religious and esthetic forms of the Middle Ages. This great tradition has been seriously weakened in the modern Western world by the success of the machine, the cult of comfort, and the illusion of perfectibility. In a materialistic culture Frank would revitalize the tradition by integrating feeling, knowing, and willing in the Person, who would then express these universal values in his actions.

Frank's hostility toward the machine extends to modern science and to empirical rationalism, but he is not so blindly or so stupidly opposed to science or to reason as some critics insist. He simply deplores the misuse of both, which permits science to produce a deadly materialistic, fragmented culture and rationalism to deny intuition or feeling. He readily admits that man needs his rational powers to control his mystical insights and his sciences to control his environment. But these utilitarian applications should be made to serve rather than to destroy "The Great Tradition."

Waldo Frank is a modern projection of the mystic tradition in American culture. His mysticism and idealism combine with his prophetic and crusading temperament to express a vision which has its inception in the Hebrew prophets and its contemporary expression in the Transcendental strain in American history. If a mechanistic and mechanical society continues to search for some meaning to justify its existence, it may yet rediscover Waldo Frank.

PAUL J. CARTER

University of Colorado
Boulder, Colorado
May 1, 1967

Acknowledgments

Grateful acknowledgment is made to the University of Pennsylvania Press for permission to quote from William Bittner, *The Novels of Waldo Frank*, copyrighted in 1955 and 1958 by William Robert Bittner; and to the Graduate School of Northwestern University and to Jerome W. Kloucek for quotations from *Waldo Frank: The Ground of His Mind and Art*, copyrighted by Jerome W. Kloucek.

Acknowledgment is also made to the following publishers for quotations from the publications named: George Braziller—*Bridgehead, The Rediscovery of Man*; Doubleday, Doran & Company—*The Bridegroom Cometh, Chart for Rough Water*; Duell, Sloan and Pearce—*The Invaders, Island in the Atlantic, The Jew in Our Day, South American Journey, Summer Never Ends, Virgin Spain* (Second Edition); Farrar & Rinehart—*In the American Jungle*; Hermitage House—*Not Heaven*; Houghton Mifflin Company—*Birth of a World*; Little, Brown and Company—*The Unwelcome Man*; Marzani & Munsell—*Cuba: Prophetic Island*; Charles Scribner's Sons—*America Hispana, City Block, Dawn in Russia, The Death and Birth of David Markand, New Year's Eve, The Re-discovery of America.*

Waldo Frank's generous assistance in making his personal notebooks and other papers available is especially appreciated. Members of the staff of the Rare Book and Manuscript Collection of the University of Pennsylvania Library were most helpful and accommodating in providing the material on deposit there.

In typing and checking the manuscript, Mrs. Ned Bowler gave valuable and efficient service. Finally, the Council on Research and Creative Work at the University of Colorado provided generous financing for this study and its important contribution is deeply appreciated.

Acknowledgments

Contents

Chronology

1889 Waldo Frank born August 25 at Long Branch, New Jersey. Grew up in the family residence on West 78th Street, New York City.

1902-1906 Attended De Witt Clinton High School in New York City.

1905 A novel, *Builders in Sand*, accepted for publication by Putnam but withdrawn by Julius Frank.

1906-1907 Attended a private preparatory school, Les Chamettes Pensionnat, in Lausanne, Switzerland.

1907-1911 Attended Yale University. Won two literary awards for essays; wrote theatrical reviews (1910-11) for New Haven *Courier-Journal*; graduated with B.A., and M.A., degrees conferred concurrently; Phi Beta Kappa; Fellow of the University.

1911 Visited ranches in Wyoming and Montana during the summer; reporter on city staff of New York *Evening Post*, October-January, 1912.

1912 Reporter for New York *Times*. Manuscript of *The Spirit of Modern French Letters* accepted by Yale University Press but withdrawn by author.

1913 Lived in Paris from February-September. Studied Bradley, Spinoza, Nietzsche, Freud.

1914 Returned to the United States; lived in Greenwich Village and elsewhere in New York City; wrote nine stories and four plays; none published. Started *The Unwelcome Man*.

1915 "The Fruit of Misadventure" published in July *Smart Set*; "Dear Little Sister-in-Law" in December *Smart Set*.

1916 Associate editor and regular contributor, *Seven Arts*, November-October, 1917. Married Margaret Naumburg, founder of the Walden School, in December.

1917 *The Unwelcome Man* published in January. Registered for the draft in June as a pacifist.

1918 *The Art of the Vieux Colombier* published. Toured Midwest and Southwest in preparing *Our America*.

1919 *Our America* published. Served as organizer for the Non-Partisan League in Kansas; worked for the Ellsworth *County Leader*; attended the League's national convention in Minneapolis.

1920 Mystical experience and "conversion" to Judaism. *The Dark Mother* published. Two tours of the South, the first with Jean Toomer.

1921 Trip to France and Spain.

1922 *Rahab* published. Son Thomas born. *City Block* published by Frank.

1923-1924 *Holiday* published. Trip to Algeria and Spain.

1924 *Salvos* published in March; *Chalk Face* in October; "For a Declaration of War" in Winter issue of *Secession.*

1925 In April began *New Yorker* profiles signed "Search-light." In November named contributing editor to *New Republic.* Translation of Jules Romains' *Lucienne* published.

1926 Divorced by Margaret Naumburg. *Virgin Spain* published. Named contributing editor to *New Masses*; trip to Cuba and the Isle of Pines with Hart Crane. *Time Exposures* published. Trip to Poland and Palestine.

1927 Married Alma Magoon. Lectured on modern art at the New School for Social Research. "Re-discovery of America" serialized in *New Republic*, December 14–September 26, 1928.

1928 *New Year's Eve* appeared in *Second American Caravan.*

1929 *Re-discovery of America* and *New Year's Eve* published as books. From July to December, lectured in Mexico, Argentina, Bolivia, Peru, Cuba; visited Chile, Colombia, Brazil, Uruguay. In December awarded Honorary Litt. D. by Universidad Nacional de San Marcos, Lima.

1930 *Primer mensaje a la América Hispana* published in Madrid. In February honored at a testimonial dinner sponsored by the Institute of International Education. Daughter Michal born.

1931 Daughter Deborah born. *America Hispana* published. Tour of Soviet Russia from August to November. Speaker at a meeting of Friends of the Soviet Union; member of committee which gathered signatures of 104 writers to protest Chinese government's persecution of Chinese writers.

1932 Chairman of Independent Miners' Relief Committee for miners in Kentucky and Tennessee. On 10 February assaulted by vigilantes and thrown out of Harlan County, Kentucky. Testified on 12 February before Senate committee investigating brutalities in Harlan County miners' strike. *Dawn In Russia* published. Headed a delegation of writers from the National Committee for the Defense of Political Prisoners protesting the treatment of the bonus marchers in Washington.

1934 *The Death and Birth of David Markand* published. Lecture tour in twelve Eastern cities. Co-editor and contributor to *America and Alfred Stieglitz.* Visited Chile, Brazil, and Argentina.

1935 As member of the International Committee for Political Prisoners, Frank filed his minority report denouncing purges in Russia. Delivered major address at the American Writers' Congress; elected first chairman of the permanent organization, the League of American Writers. Delegate to the Paris meeting of the International Congress of Writers in Defence of Culture.

1936 Resigned from the League of American Writers. Political activities as member of the Committee of Professional Groups for Browder and Ford. Traveled with Browder during his campaign for President. Headed the American Society for Technical Aid to Spanish Democracy.

1937 American representative and invited guest of the Congress of Revolutionary Writers and Artists of Mexico in Mexico City. Traveled and lectured in Mexico. *In the American Jungle* published. Severed relations with the Communist Party and left for a year in Europe.

1938 *The Bridegroom Cometh* published in London.

1939 Guest of the national government of Mexico in May–June. Toured southern provinces with President Cárdenas. *The Bridegroom Cometh* published in New York.

1940 *Chart for Rough Water* published. Resigned as contributing editor to *New Republic.*

1941 Addressed the international conference of the New Education Fellowship in Ann Arbor, Michigan. *Summer Never Ends* published.

1942 Revised edition of *Virgin Spain* published. Second Latin American lecture tour in Brazil, Argentina, Chile, Uruguay, Peru, Colombia. Assaulted by Fascists in Buenos Aires. *Ustedes y Nosotros* published in Buenos Aires. Honored at a testimonial dinner sponsored by Union for Democratic Action.

1943 *South American Journey* published. Divorced from Alma Magoon and married Jean Klempner.

1944 *The Jew in Our Day* published.

1945 Member of the Committee on Peace Problems, a subcommittee of the American Jewish Congress.
1946 *Island in the Atlantic* published.
1947 Delivered a hundred lectures on a coast-to-coast tour of the United States. Son Jonathan Waldo born.
1948 *The Invaders* published. Trip to Venezuela, Colombia, Ecuador, Bolivia, and Peru to do research on Bolivar for the biography commissioned by the Venezuelan government.
1949 Named Honorary Professor by the Central University of Ecuador.
1951 *Birth of a World* published.
1952 Elected to membership in the National Institute of Arts and Letters.
1953 *Not Heaven* published.
1954 Began a monthly syndicated series of critical essays for Latin American periodicals. Son Timothy born.
1957 *Bridgehead* published.
1958 *The Rediscovery of Man* published.
1959 Traveled to Europe, Mexico, Cuba.
1960 "A Regular Fellow" rejected by nine publishers. Temporary chairman of the Fair Play for Cuba Committee. Resigned as contributor of syndicated series of essays to Latin America because of his pro-Castro position.
1961 *Cuba: Prophetic Island* published.
1967 Died January 9 in White Plains, New York.

Waldo Frank

CHAPTER 1

Creation is Revolution

"IN A DYING WORLD, creation is revolution." This closing sentence of *Our America* (1919) states the two premises upon which Waldo Frank builds his career as a man of letters. Western civilization has been slowly dying since the Renaissance, its life-giving spiritual heritage strangling in materialism and rationalism; only a revolutionary kind of creativity in thought and act can thwart the decay. "We must break our impotent habit of constant issuance into petty deed," Frank warns. "We must begin to generate within ourselves the energy which is love of life. For that energy, to whatever form the mind consign it, is religious. Its act is creation."[1]

Frank started generating this energy while he was still young by rebelling mildly against the comfortable middle-class world of his parents and by determining to become a writer whose words "shall be proofs of God." His reading—he read over a thousand books before entering college—revealed to him Balzac, Tolstoi, Poe, Thoreau, and most important of all, Whitman and Spinoza. These writers led him beyond the mild moralistic secularism of his parents into more revolutionary political and religious speculations. He did not formalize his beliefs until later, of course, when they became the philosophical point of view in every book he wrote; but it is necessary to have at least a general idea of them before one considers his individual works.

As noted in the Preface, organic wholeness summarizes Frank's concept of existence. The universe is an ordered, unified entity underlying all religion, science, and art. God is not a personal deity but the apex of collective consciousness. No one has existence apart from this consciousness; each individual is capable of transcending his binding ego by being "overwhelmed," as Frank describes the experience in one of his personal notebooks, "by the awareness that God IS," and thereby becoming a true Person. Such an awareness requires a kind of revolutionary creativity in thought and action, for it can materialize only through a creative perception of the organic wholeness behind the seeming fragmentation of life.

I *Ethical Culture*

Waldo Frank grew up in a comfortable middle-class world shaped largely by the bourgeois culture of his family and his environment. His father, Julius J. Frank, was born in New York City on March 3, 1852, to German Jewish immigrants. A prototype of the American success story, Julius Frank prospered as a lawyer and by the 1880's had an office near Wall Street and a four-story brownstone in the middle of a street of row-houses on West 78th in the area between Columbus Circle and Columbia University. As the American attorney for the Hamburg-Amerika Line, Julius Frank went to Europe almost every year; and his son remembered the long letters which made the cities his father described live vividly for the boy. Several times before he was old enough for college, Waldo accompanied his father and traveled in the lands which he had read about in his father's library, a room which was, he recalls, "a sanctuary of Europe."[2]

Waldo's mother also contributed to this European "nature" of his boyhood. Helene Rosenberg Frank came from the Alabama branch of a Jewish clan of international business men. Her father, a blockade runner during the Civil War, established in Reconstruction times the Standard Varnish Company in New York City. Mrs. Frank, a talented musician, was accompanied at the organ or the piano by her husband as she sang Beethoven, Brahms, Schubert, Schumann, bringing "the lands across the sea miraculously near" to the boy huddled on the stair to his fourth-floor room. Years later, in 1941, when his mother died, Frank wrote in Notebook XV: "My mother was two beings. Deep, she was an artist: a generous, intuitive, imaginative artist. In extension (more dimensionally than this 'depth' of her) she was a woman of her world, class, generation. This was the woman who ordinarily functioned. . . . Intellectually, we were far apart. . . ."

The Franks did not observe Jewish ritual, but Julius Frank was a trustee of the Society for Ethical Culture, his compromise with his Jewish heritage. A Jeffersonian Democrat, he was active in reform organizations opposed to Tammany, among them the Committee of Seventy. Waldo describes his father as "an imperious, passionate man, whose prime passion was respect for the personality of others. A tyrant in matters of deportment, he hated all interference in adventures of the spirit." Waldo's spirit tested his father's patience severely. Yet Julius Frank's "respect for the personality of others" made it possible for his son to devote his life to writing.

Fortunately for young Waldo there were other children in the family; two girls—Edna, who died during Waldo's youth, and Enid—and an older brother, Joseph. Waldo, youngest of the children, was the rebel. He did not agree with his family on much, and he was aggressively iconoclastic in religion, politics, and art. Members of the family were remarkably patient and tolerant, especially his father, who seems to have understood his opponent well enough to be capable of constructive compromises.

Waldo Frank was a brilliant but trying student at De Witt Clinton High School. He was captain of the debating team and associate editor of both the yearbook and the literary magazine. For the annual oratory contest in 1905 he "harangued the audience about the merits of an unknown, dead poet called Walt Whitman," and was awarded a gold medal for his effort. In his senior year he refused to attend English class because he knew more about Shakespeare than his teacher. The principal was willing to waive disciplinary action if Waldo would return to the class, but he persisted in his refusal and did not graduate. Julius Frank quietly and graciously accepted this impetuous action, possibly because his son had already passed the entrance examinations for Harvard and had had a long novel, *Builders in the Sand*, accepted for publication by G. P. Putnam. (The father, however, wisely withdrew the novel when he learned that it was to be handled as a "stunt.")

Waldo's rebellious behavior, on the other hand, may have prompted his father's decision to let him mature a bit before he was allowed to enter college. After the family spent the summer in Europe, Julius Frank placed Waldo in Les Chamettes Pensionnat in Lausanne, Switzerland. There he studied French intensively and read widely in French literature while he continued his lessons on the cello. His knowledge of and devotion to music, his mother's contribution to his development, is reflected throughout his later writings, especially in the form of his novels.

Given this European orientation, young Waldo quickly became enchanted with European student life: "I consorted with students from every land of Europe. . . . They were not 'pretty' fellows. They knew life—women—books . . . . all the old dwellers of the books . . . in my father's library took on flesh, grew warm, grew urgent." He considered becoming a peripatetic student. Curious about German academic life, he decided to enroll in Heidelberg. But brother Joseph proved less philosophical than the indulgent father: "You are not going to Heidelberg," said my brother. "You are going to be an American, by gum! And what's more, you are not going to Harvard. You're queer enough as it is. You're going to be . . . as *human* an American as I can make you. I'm going to send you to a place that will smooth out your angles and your crotchets. Yale for you."

II *Whiffenpoof*

Waldo Frank admits that he "went through college a rather cantankerous rebel." His classmates, more engrossed in football, fraternities, and sentiment than in ideas, revolutionary movements, and Nietzsche, "seemed children" to him. (Quincy Burt's anti-social career at Yale, as narrated in *The Unwelcome Man,* Frank's first published novel, is not a literal account of the author's life at college, but it suggests something of his isolation and aspirations.) Waldo's student essays were rejected by the college publications, probably to remind him of his place, because two of them later won literary awards. He played cello with the university orchestra, and in his last year wrote reviews of plays for the New Haven *Courier-Journal*, reviews which were usually scornful of America's woeful "lack of culture." Occasionally, he took Professors William E. Hocking or William Lyon Phelps with him to the theater. (Later Frank wrote a patronizing sketch of Phelps for the *New Yorker*, which hurt "Billy" deeply. Although an accurate criticism of the professor's deficiencies as a literary critic, Frank regretted his cruel commentary.)

Frank's major academic interest was the drama, especially the French. A notebook, dated 1908, lists his reading. There are 1,043 titles recorded, and in a note at the end of the list he deplores not having started his listing earlier since "it omits those years preceding in which I really did my most ravenous and fundamental reading. For, from fifteen to nineteen, I read more books in a year than is equalled in any year ensuing."

During his college career he read widely in modern fiction and, of course, in drama. His reading of French plays led to the writing of his second unpublished book, *The Spirit of Modern French Letters.* The manuscript was accepted by Yale University Press in March, 1912; but by then Frank was busy in other activities, and when he returned to the book he found that many of his opinions had changed. (The wrapper around the manuscript, now preserved in the Waldo Frank papers in the Rare Book and Manuscript Collection of the University of Pennsylvania Library, has this scrawled notation: "Withdrawn by author as he ceased to share its convictions.") He did not, however, change his mind about the critical point of view expressed in the Introduction attacking "the great gulf of ignorance" revealed in "the Anglo-Saxon idea of French Immorality," which blocks appreciation of French literature: "Convince the intelligent speaker of English that Zola is not all filth, Baudelaire not a degenerate and the dramas of Henry Becque anything but a wallowing in concentrated muck, and his ready mind will soon seek out for itself" a way of appreciating literary styles which differ in form and method.

Having completed his work for the bachelor's degree in three years, Waldo stayed at Yale to graduate with his class, receiving the bachelor's and master's degrees together in 1911. In addition to winning the two literary awards, he was made an honorary fellow of the college (Professor Phelps arranged that) and a member of Phi Beta Kappa.

After his graduation, Frank got his first glimpse of America beyond the Hudson, visiting as a paying guest the ranches of college friends in Wyoming and Montana during the summer of 1911. In the fall he returned to New York planning to become a drama critic and to write plays. For three months he was a reporter on the New York *Evening Post*; then he moved to the *Times*, where he remained until January, 1913, when he was fired for writing a story for which the paper was sued.

But work as a reporter did not satisfy his compulsion to become a writer. Although he left home and took a furnished room, he still could not find the time or stimulation necessary for his apprenticeship in literature. Once again Paris beckoned: "New York seemed wholly body. . . . A vast town, New York; but since it was concerned only with the mechanics of sheer physical growth, it struck me as a baby. . . . I could not accept this gross, this infantile America. . . . Being a child myself, I made the same old gross mistake; I imagined that my Paradise existed 'over there,' across the sea. I . . . went to live in Paris."

There he found the congenial atmosphere which had already captured Eliot, Pound, and Gertrude Stein; but he did not share their sense of alienation and sought instead, as he recalls later, "men after my own heart" in the French literary world. He began to write intensively, mostly plays; but his notebook for the period has sketches of many themes for stories, most of which, however, are about New York. He also started serious study of Bradley, Spinoza, Nietzsche, and Freud; the philosophy of Spinoza eventually became the major influence upon his thinking.

He remained in Paris for eight months, from February to September, 1913, happy and busy: "I found myself in a world where writing—the sheer creative act—was considered a sacrament and a service: . . . It was in the air—this rhythm of creation. Life was looked on as a lovely, mysterious adventure, and its true priests were they who . . . revealed its beauty." Then, just as he began to feel truly at home, he returned to the States: "I gave it up quite simply because I did not want it, and I could not stand it. . . . I was being nourished by what other men . . . had created. I was a parasite." The expatriates' sneering criticisms of America had only sharpened his need to go back home: "If what they said was true, all the more urgent was the return of men like themselves . . . who could endow America with what they accused America of lacking."

CHAPTER 2

Beginnings

UPON HIS RETURN to New York, Frank took a room in Washington Place in order to share in the life of Greenwich Village. He found his country "a hostile waste, consumed by the fires of possession." But the hard lot of the artist in America in 1914 only proved how much he was needed. Fortunately, he had the money to finance his campaign for publication. He hired an agent, had his plays typed and copyrighted, and bombarded magazines and producers with his creations. Of the nine stories and four plays written in 1913, none was published, although one play, *The Key*, was accepted in 1915 by Alla Nazimova for vaudeville, and after she dropped it, by Helen Freeman's Nine O'Clock Theater in 1916—but it was not produced. Frank's first publication was a short article about the musician Leo Ornstein, which appeared in *The Outlook*, April, 1915, to be followed by a long story, "The Fruit of Misadventure" in *Smart Set* (July, 1915). Meanwhile, he had nearly finished "The Sisters," a sequence of four novelettes, each a study of a woman, each portraying a different type, and each showing a variation in mood. One of these, "Dear Little Sister-in-Law," was published in *Smart Set* (December, 1915). But the sequence found no publisher, although Sinclair Lewis, a reader for Doran, saw the potentialities in Frank's use of the new psychology, and encouraged him to try another novel.

I *Ishmael*

The new novel was already underway. *The Unwelcome Man* (written in 1914 and 1915 but not published until January, 1917, after fourteen publishers had rejected it) is almost a case study in Freudian psychology of "the common child . . . who does not emerge at all and whose talent disappears."[1] The "common child" is Quincy Burt, the eighth offspring and the fifth son of a struggling surveyor living on Long Island at the turn of the century. Upon Quincy's arrival, the bitter father invests in twin beds and pointedly sets out to ignore the new baby.

Part One of the novel—the childhood and adolescence of the unwelcome man—tells of Quincy's painful discovery of his rejection not only by his father but by his equally insensitive family, excepting only the beaten, ineffectual mother. The author attempts—unsuccessfully—to enter the emotional world of the child during his first year and to experiment fitfully with the Oedipus complex.

> From his father, indeed, the infant came to feel a new quality of apartness. . . . And it was not long ere infantile wisdom had sensed the truth.
> . . . . His father alone——like him——lived with no deeper source. And between them, needed by them both, claimed by them both, was this delicious creature of sweet embrace and warm bestowal! There lay the kernel of all bitterness. For Quincy felt with the fibre of his being, that his mother was not completely, not exclusively his own. . . .
> Fully and spendidly, he came to hate his father. . . .

The characters, especially the father, are overdrawn almost to the extremes of melodrama, so that they exist only as stereotypes in the painful emotional world of a youth awakening to rejection. The melodramatic tone is intensified by the experiences of this drab family: the oldest boy falls off a roof and is crippled for life, and he exists thereafter as a dour, satanic figure in the world of Quincy; two of the father's favorites die of scarlet fever, thereby accentuating his bitterness toward Quincy; the family is lifted from its desperate economic plight only by the fortuitous discovery of a rich vein of metal on some Wyoming land the father had bought in the hope of his youth.

Part Two is concerned with Quincy's college years and the intensification of his isolation. His struggle is personified in the conflicting personalities of Professor Deering, who represents an appeal to Quincy's mind and to his idealistic nature, and the professor's wife, who seduces him in his first experience of love. Confused and disillusioned by reality, he turns savagely against his dreams and all that nurtures them; he quits college and surrenders to the world of business where unity is a simple by-product of making money.

In Part Three Quincy is unable to find a meaningful identity with the world. In the college section of the novel he had failed to make himself welcome because of the flaw in his own nature: "Quincy lacked soul-endurance. The part of him that should have fired his acts seemed scant of fuel. And from this want had come a timidness of purpose. . . . Not only in the face of opposition . . . but in the effort of accomplishment. . . . Quincy's own suffering . . . was to be indissolubly set in the suffering he helped to cause in others." Now when he tries to establish contact with a broader world, represented by his business office, by his romance with a girl as bound in social activities as a business man in commerce, and by a New York which repulses him, he again cannot find the strength for growth—or for suicide. He can only lose himself among the living dead floating on the turbid stream of the city: "All that remained to seal his brotherhood was to forget even . . . that he was dead, to walk the way blankly, blindly. . . ."

The difficulty in *The Unwelcome Man* is one that plagues the subsequent novels: the protagonist is an abstraction; his struggles are shadowy projections of psychological twists of mind. There is too much of the prig in Quincy to win the reader's identification. He is an intellectualization of the author's concept of adolescence. Frank seems aware of this defect in characterization in his analysis of Quincy's failure:

> He did not know how cowardice had betrayed him in the guise of loyalty and virtue, and how the very subtle plea of the herd had filled his ears, edging him on to serve it and deny himself, give up to it his treasures, in hope of some vague interest which the herd proclaimed as duty and morality and good. . . . For he did not guess that, behind it all, lay the fear of venturing alone, the fear of being a measure to himself and of wielding his life as his life's measure. He did not dare to dream that there was in him, glorying itself, the ancient, leprous fear of the herd's children to graze outside of the herd's shadow.

Quincy is the unwelcome man because he is neither true to himself nor to the herd. This duality, Frank seems to say, is responsible for the failure of the individual to find the harmony, the identity, with the pattern symbolized in nature.

Despite its flaws, *The Unwelcome Man* is a useful introduction to Waldo Frank's writing. In consciously using Freudian psychology and the interior monologue in the narrative, he is a forerunner in the development of the psychological novel.[2] Thereafter, the psychology of all his characters will proceed from the unconscious as they struggle to find their identity and the meaning of life.

That struggle, however, is not limited to the psychological; it also involves the social. Quincy Burt is every man of spiritual instincts who finds himself unwelcome in a materialistic society. The business world is a bloodless substitute for life; the city is a horror: "The hammering monotony of huge buildings that were neither beautiful . . . nor useful . . . monuments of vanity and folly . . . ; the fetid subways . . . cesspools that stunk . . . ; the spiritless cafés . . . : the unending blight of magazines and journals—made from the crushing of fair forests into wood-pulp! . . . And the mad misery of the dwellers!—proud to be smothered in the biggest subway, proud to be cheated in the biggest stores, proud to be lied to by the biggest journals, proud to be sheep in the biggest pen!" This revolt against the city becomes, of course, a characteristic theme of the novelists of the 1920's.

In the reasons for Quincy's failure, Waldo Frank is also groping toward the mystical philosophy which characterizes his esthetic and his social criticism. Quincy cannot sense the unity of all things; he cannot identify himself with the whole: "And until each man has sharpened his instrument for vision within himself, there is no need in his decrying, or attempting to reform, the frauds and mockeries of government and church and public utterance. . . . He who clears the eyes of one child toward itself does more for the truth than the leader of a national rebellion. And until there be a nation made up of men who were just such children, all reform and all revolt must be a romantic variant upon some theme of falsehood."

The "vision within," to anticipate Frank's full expression of it years later, is the awareness of organic wholeness, the consciousness of one's place in the universe because of his intuitive sense of the presence of the cosmic in him. This consciousness, however,

> . . . involves recognition of being partial—existing only in relation to all other persons and all other things—and at the same time involves recognition of God—not fragmented, but entire—within oneself. The Person aware of God within him does not live "in terms of the part as if it were the whole," but "in terms of the Whole expressed through its parts." If God is within the Person, God can be within the People, and achievement of harmony in a society—harmony within itself and harmony with other societies —involves the same awareness on the part of a people.[3]

This concept is a major theme in Frank's novels and in his cultural studies, and its gradual formulation is a useful index to his career.

II *Editor*

Frank completed *The Unwelcome Man* in 1915, but he did not start work on his second novel until 1918. His appointment as associate editor of the new *Seven Arts* magazine in the fall of 1916 reduced his creative activity, although he continued to write short stories and articles, ten of them for the magazine.

He was an industrious and resourceful editor; Van Wyck Brooks, who was closely associated with the publication, says that "Waldo Frank was the real creator of *The Seven Arts*."[4] For the first issue Frank wrote an article on Sherwood Anderson, in which he not only recognized the potential greatness of Anderson, whose *Windy McPherson's Son* had just been published, but also expressed the core of his and the magazine's literary point of view:

> . . . our artists have been of two extremes: those who gained an almost unbelievable purity of expression by the very violence of their self-isolation, and those who, plunging into the American maelstrom, were submerged in it, lost their vision altogether, and gave forth a gross chronicle and a blind cult of the American Fact.
>
> The significance of Sherwood Anderson . . . is simply that he has escaped these two extremes, that he suggests at last a presentation of life shot through with the searching color of truth, which is a signal for a native culture.[5]

Unfortunately for the arts in America, the magazine folded with its twelfth number. Although Frank claimed later that the "mutual distrusts and spiritual failures" of the individuals of the group killed it,[6] World War I was the primary cause. The magazine had taken a pacifist position—Frank later registered for the draft as a conscientious objector "to this War and not because of pacifist or religious views"[7]—and financial support was withdrawn from the enterprise. Before its last issue in October, 1917, Frank was stricken by an illness that was incorrectly diagnosed as appendicitis and an unnecessary operation nearly killed him. He did not fully recover until September, 1918, but he had not been idle during his convalescence. He started work on his second novel, *The Dark Mother*; toured the West in preparation for his first cultural study, *Our America*; and wrote a long essay, *The Art of the Vieux Colombier*.

III *French Theater*

Frank first heard of the work of Jacques Copeau and the *Théâtre du Vieux Colombier* during his days in Paris, and he had written about them in *Seven Arts* when the company performed in New York during the war. His subsequent history and analysis of the Copeau theater expresses some of his early theories about art and culture. Such an experimental theater is possible only in an organic society like that of France, "for the tradition of French art is revolution: . . ."[8] The artist does not have to struggle, as in the United States, against an indifferent or hostile environment. In France, "wherever one touches her, one is in contact with her entire life." And since France is also the center of other cultures, other peoples, one is also "in contact as well with Europe." Since no artistic movement is primarily intellectual but expands emotionally, "the distinctive quality of the Vieux Colombier . . . lies precisely in its emotional and unconscious—its *organic* coming into being." New York "thirsts after the revelation and salvation of a dramatic faith."

Publication of the essay as a small paper-bound book by the *Nouvelle Revue Française* not only won Frank an enthusiastic audience in France but also led to his writing his first book-length cultural study, *Our America.* Two of the leaders of the French propaganda expedition to the United States, Jacques Copeau and Gaston Gallimard, the Director of the publishing house of the *Nouvelle Revue Française,* having heard Frank express his thoughts about his own country, asked him "to write a book to make America known to France."[9]

IV *America Discovered*

Frank wisely decided not to compose a history or a lecture for France but to talk to his countrymen, to express for them the promise and the dream of America which had not yet been realized; for America is "a conception to be created: . . . a step in consciousness," which can only be taken by a young, articulate generation "in revolt against the academies and institutions which would whittle America down to a few stale realities current fifty years ago . . . . that organized anarchy to-day expressed in Industrialism which would deny to America any life ——hence any unity at all——beyond the ties of traffic and the arteries of trade."

The quest for consciousness gives the book its unifying theme;

the object of the quest is a richer, fuller life, one which will embrace all experience and at the same time bring man an awareness of his link with the cosmos. In other words, man must rediscover his religious sense, the requisite of any healthy culture. It is this mystic, spiritual awareness which has been stunted, sublimated, ignored in the winning of America: "The spiritual power is man's capacity to feel life as a whole. It is that part of us which dwells within and yet may merge us with the world. The pioneer had brought such power with him: . . . It languished for lack of nurture."

The pioneering phase of American life was necessarily a repressive process in which "every narrowing instinct of self-preservation and acquisition tended to make them [the pioneers] intolerant, materialistic, unaesthetic." The colonist had no time for vision, for beauty, no need "to consult either his social or his spiritual senses." Church and school became utilitarian; "culture," an appendage of wealth, even a business asset. Pragmatism, whose measure of value is utility, developed as a natural corollary of a materialistic conception of progress and further stultified the spiritual force necessary for the creation of a new reality. "For, while the American was active in the external world——mature and conscious there——his starved inner life stunted his spiritual powers . . . to the dream-dimensions of the infant."

Frank selects writers and artists to illustrate the failure—and, later in the book, the hope—of America, since its statesmen after Lincoln, who was "one of the first of the prophets of a more vivid, religious American world," exemplify only decadence, as Theodore Roosevelt and Woodrow Wilson. In Chapter One the pioneer's strict utilitarianism accounts for the "infantile romanticism" of Jack London and Mark Twain, which hid their despair. *Huckleberry Finn* is a great work; however, it is not "the expression of a rich national culture like the books of Chaucer, Rabelais, Cervantes, but . . . the voice of American chaos, the voice of a precultural epoch." Twain had a great soul, but he did not believe in it; and "the clown tragedy of Mark Twain is prelude to the American drama." (Here Frank anticipates the theme of Van Wyck Brooks' *The Ordeal of Mark Twain*, published in 1920.)

In America the pioneer and the Puritan became one as the latter suppressed his religious impulses: "The Puritan movement was simply a chapter in the long history of religious decadence."

The Puritan wanted power. To get it, he conserved and concentrated his energy through his austere way of life and then, under the pressure of pioneering, channelled it into the outer world of material affairs. "Materialism was an invisible Magnet toward which each element of New England thought and life needed to point." Morality, sobriety, and thrift were aids to commercial progress and powerful adjuncts of capitalism. Thus did New England establish a material culture which was to become that of the United States.

The desire for the "completed consciousness"—the spiritual—did not die in New England, as it did in the pioneering West; it simply became Transcendental in writers like Emerson and fled the "magnetized reality." Emerson's dualism supplies the rationalization which a materialistic culture needed: "The hypocrisy of the American who goes to church on Sunday and bleeds his brother Monday, who leads a sexually vicious life and insists on 'pure' books . . . who preaches liberty and democracy and free-speech, and supports the subtlest Oligarchy of modern times, found support by a bitter irony in the books of this pure spirit." Poe's imagination, finding no home in Puritan America, escaped into exoticism; Henry James—"a strange sort of monster . . . with vast peripheral development and no depths"—fled the country and gave his small vitality "to the creation of a world rootless like himself." The Puritan ethos triumphed.

Like the Puritans, "another chosen People," the Jews, slowly repressed their spiritual sense in their almost "frenzied conformation to the land of . . . new opportunity." Since in 1919 there were only about three million Jews in the United States—one third of them in New York City—their cultural influence would not justify a chapter in *Our America* were it not for the symbolic significance of their spiritual impoverishment by the same dream of power that corrupted the Puritan. For, like the Puritan, the Jew "played a rôle in the building of America out of all proportion to his numerical strength, because . . . he was strategically placed," and because he did everything with more intensity than his fellows. In order to subdue his mystical yearnings, however, he becomes a modern phenomenon—"the anaesthetic Jew," who instinctively declares defensive war against any spiritual or esthetic approach which might stir the senses he denies. So Jews like Julius Frank tried to solve their religious problem with The Society for Ethical Culture, a completely commercialized religion, and "in the American chaos the Jew went under." But the

Jew will rise again in a new America which can be created through the rejection of empirical thought and the recognition of the place of art and religion in a dynamic culture.

Chapter Four of the book is a transitional one where Frank contrasts the epitome of sterile materialism, Southern California, with Indian-Mexican cultures which, though doomed, still symbolize dramatically the creative power of harmony with Nature and the mysterious forces surrounding it. Los Angeles in 1919 has no direction. Like the California orange, it offers only bigness without flavor. Southern California reflects the inner poverty of the pioneer when there are no more frontiers to conquer and he is thrown back upon himself. The Indian, on the other hand, "sought happiness in harmony with his surroundings: sought life by cultivation, rather than exploitation." The union of the Indian and the Spaniard created a native culture, but "the Mexican is already lost in the spell of the tin-can and the lithograph." The richness of these "buried cultures" suggests, however, the way to a new synthesis which will redeem the promise of America.

The next three chapters of *Our America* develop the counter theme to the negations of the first three—the signs of the coming synthesis. Even in Chicago, symbol of the chaos of industrial America, the voices of the "uprising generation" already express the one thing needed in the land: "inherent life." Writers like Carl Sandburg, Sherwood Anderson, and Frederick Booth "disclose the luminosity of American materials," and "the glory of truth is but the glory of *being*." Such artists represent the hope of creating spiritual values out of chaos.

In New England the still, small "yea" to life in the Puritan world, "first voiced by Thoreau," is heard again in Albert Pinkham Ryder, "the great American painter," Robert Frost, Amy Lowell, and Henry Adams. *The Education of Henry Adams,* which sums the significance, tragedy, and promise of New England, is also a cry for new gods. Having said "yea" to existence, the new voices may bring life even to New England.

New York City is the climax of our "extraverted" land; its weary, sodden masses are caught in a machine, are joyless, spiritless, lifeless, devoid of "that inner light which can alone illumine." There are, however, two potential life-giving forces pouring into the city: the young would-be artists and writers who have left town and farm to create a different world for themselves; and the "thought of Europe," brought by cable and traveler, with the new incentives of revolt and rebirth. Already there are new leaders. Alfred Stieglitz, "the one major American in art," makes details of industrialism "serve the unifying vision of human spirit." He with Leo Ornstein and Paul Rosenfeld in music and James Oppenheim in poetry mark the renaissance of the Jew in his new land. Critics like Mencken, Hackett, Clarence Day and essayists like Van Wyck Brooks and Randolph Bourne give promise of a new beginning.

The magnitude of the challenge to create a new America is revealed in Chapter Eight, in which Frank compares the "ignorance, flatulence, complacency" of the "herd" with the multitudes of whom Whitman dreamed. "The one true hierarchy of values in the world is the hierarchy of Consciousness." The great mystics, like Whitman, possess the highest consciousness, which sees mundane life as an elementary part of the organic whole. Whitman offers the vision of spiritual progress to the multitudes now enslaved and enfeebled by the machine and its control of press, church, school, and theater. Only when the herd hears the voice of the poet and the artist will a vision like Whitman's be realized.

What will be necessary to win the future are religion and revolution. Material, mechanical life has deluged man's mind with fact and detail.

> Only the thought and deed which lead man to the sources of life are the life-givers. Broken from these conduits, he becomes the most helpless of particles in a buffeting world. His superior mental scope serves merely to destroy him. For it lets in an infinitude of facts, and . . . they overwhelm him. Only in the consciousness of life as a Whole . . . his feet upon earth and his head piercing the skies——the consciousness which all religions in their own ways preserve, all arts express——can man prevail against the clutter of a factual and emotional multiverse.

The beauty and strength of America have been trampled by the march of materialism. The cumulative press of affairs and the vestiges of the Puritan philosophy have produced as oppressive a system as that of Russia under the Czars. America's success has meant suppression of life. "The man who dreamed, loved, created rather than possessed, was a byword and a pariah." But now "the soil stands ready to be turned." Only the creative impulse is needed. It cannot, however, be merely intellectual; it must be spiritual, must proceed from love—"Love of life, love of *being*." It is this love—religious and esthetic—which supplies, when applied to practical demands through suffering and experience, the dynamic energy of revolt. American energy has become external instead of internal and is therefore expended wholly in pioneering and exploiting, so that the American no longer has the inner resources and spiritual substance required for the re-creating of a world. Only by throwing off the tyranny of the material and by developing the creative energy of love of life will the American be able to find and use the source of true power: "For that energy, to whatever form the mind consign it, is religious. Its act is creation. And in a dying world, creation is revolution."

Our America is the product of such an act of creation, and its religious fervor helped to inspire the revolutionary spirit of the 1920's. The book was published in November, 1919, by the new and adventurous publishing house of Boni and Liveright. (The French and British editions appeared a year later.) It had a great reception, coming at just the right time to attract the various postwar groups concerned with new ideas in opposition to the stereotyped thinking of the so-called "practical men" of a materialistic society. It resumed the cultural battles begun in the *Seven Arts* by speaking challengingly to groping young artists of a new conception of the promise of America. One of those young artists, Gorham Munson, remembered vividly the impact of *Our America*:

> The book dazzled my immediate generation. . . . We were then two or three years out of college and more recently out of military service. We had taken no course in American literature; . . . We felt obstructed by puritanism in expression of our vision and interpretation of life. Puritanism in the guise of Comstockery was a rampant force and had suppressed Dreiser's "The Genius" on incredibly Nice-Nellyish grounds. Prohibition—which was overt, crusading puritanism—loomed before us. We were "sort of socialistic." . . . We had also read Freud's *Interpretation of Dreams* and were very hopeful for the advance of psychology. . . .
>
> We had no grasp of our national letters. Mark Twain? We thought of him as a buffoon who amused our parents against whom we were rebelling. Melville was in limbo. We had begun to read Whitman. . . . *The Little Review*, . . . the *Nation*, and the *New Republic*. . . .
>
> . . . We were ready for eloquence on the promise and the dream of America. Waldo Frank came swiftly to proclaim promise and dream, and his was the voice that spoke thrillingly of a conception of America to be created by the young writers and artists. . . .

> *Our America* had a powerful negative argument about our culture, and the young people who read the work applauded it. . . .
>
> . . . Frank heralded the men who had found new gods to serve, the men who represented the promise of America. . . .
>
> . . . this inspiring book bore out the motto from Walt Whitman that preceded its text: "I say that the real and permanent grandeur of These States must be their Religion. . . ."
>
> Fit words for the prologue to the great year of 1920![10]

Nearly half a century after its publication, *Our America* is still an appealing and stirring book; its zestful spirit offsets its immature, oversimplified judgments; its version of the American Dream remains as challenging as ever. But it is also useful as an introduction to the religious and esthetic principles which appear throughout Frank's subsequent writing, especially in his cultural studies. It is in this book, for example, that Frank discovers in the American Southwest a culture that will eventually lead him to Spain and to Latin America in quest of America.

The style in which *Our America* is written, on the other hand, is least representative of Frank's characteristic prose, which is more rhetorical, polished, and complex. There is in the rhythms of this book a kind of urgency, or emotional drive, which finds its outlet in vivid imagery, epigrammatic sentences, and dynamic, short paragraphs. Image and epigram continue in Frank's mature style, but the tone becomes more philosophical and reflective, the rhythms less compelling.

V *Turning Point*

In November, 1919, after checking the proofs of *Our America,* Frank set out on a tour of the Middle West and South to relax and to plan his next move. He remained almost a month in Osage City and Ellsworth, Kansas, writing propaganda editorials for the Ellsworth *County Leader* and working as an organizer for Arthur Townley's Non-Partisan League, a socialist-front attempt to revive the old Populist vote.[11] Like David Markand, who is the hero of one of the major novels, Frank discovered in this Midwest setting the folk of America. Impressed by their idealism and strength of character, he was bitterly disillusioned by the actions of their political representatives at the St. Paul convention of the League, who cynically sold out their followers in return for personal power. Frank wrote Sherwood Anderson on December 18, 1919: ". . . here, projected, was the Socialist State that is coming next . . . . it will be quite as far from thee & me, quite as ignorant of us & quite as hostile to our gods, as Tammany Hall. Let it come. . . . For it will at best, perhaps, more decently apportion food and sunlight. But let us know it for what it is. Let us be brave and admit that political representation will *always, must* always be a game for the trickey, the brutal. . . ."[12]

After this experience, Frank returned briefly to New York in January, 1920, and then wandered down to Richmond, Virginia, to brood over his career and his personal problems. His four-year marriage to Margaret Naumburg, the founder of the Walden School in New York City, was breaking up; and he had not written anything for seven months, although he had tried to work on the final revision of his second novel, *The Dark Mother*, which he had started the previous year. Spiritually, he was groping for some sense of direction, for a personal awareness of his place in the universe. His reading in the medieval Jewish mystics and in Spinoza had led him to question his youthful rejection of Judaism, and he wondered if he could now accept a faith which he had once easily dismissed because of his father's attitude.

His answer came in the form of three mystical experiences during February, 1920, while he was still in Richmond. He gave a literal description of these visitations in a notebook with the title, *Sights*, and with this summarizing preface: "Scattered Notes of Thought and Vision Placed here at Random for my own Guidance at such Time . . . when I feel readier to write *The Jewish Word*—my Own Confession of Jewish Consciousness which came to me in the year 1920: Making me Know Myself at last Part of a Vast Human Drama, a Transcendant Mystery—the Contemporary in a Way Terribly Intense of Spinoza, Philo, Jesus, Jeremiah. . . ." This mystical intuition of oneness finally gives meaning to his, and mankind's, suffering: "It is the perfect passion and Glory which are life that become in the imperfect man the tissue and agony of living. Rejoice therefore in thy Crucifixion, for it is Life that God inflicts upon thee. There is no destruction save in hate, no death save in denial. Lift thyself up to Love, and thou wilt live."

At the same time, he found renewed justification for resuming his writing career; he recorded in the notebook his new dedication: "My will, O God, to create is good since I do know it must be fulfilled through Love. . . . O God, save me to create by making me now to love this world that must be the material of my creation . . even the material of my love." The immediate effect was a spurt of creativity. Within two months he completed the revision of *The Dark Mother*, the first draft of *City Block*, and the first part of *Rahab*.

VI *David Markand Arrives*

Frank's second novel to be published, *The Dark Mother* (October, 1920), is more closely related to *The Unwelcome Man* in form and style than to *City Block* or to *Rahab*; but it shares with the last two books an increase in the mystical element in Frank's writing after his personal revelation. In one sense *The Dark Mother* is a continuation of *The Unwelcome Man*; it is concerned with the psychological problems involved in growing up, in finding one's true self and one's relation to life. Its protagonist, David Markand, who appears in subsequent novels, is nineteen, "the boy who was nearly a man"; but his struggle, unlike Quincy Burt's, is not with his family but with those who try to capture his spirit. From the beginning, David is confronted by the manipulations of an older companion, Tom Rennard, who represents the successful yet cynical man of the modern world —the kind of satanic stereotype of charm and corruption who appears in nearly half of Frank's novels to challenge the saintly heroes.

The lives of David and Tom become entangled as the latter seeks a homosexual relationship which he thinks will create a reality and meaning that he cannot find in his activities as a highly successful lawyer. Thus the novel becomes a psychological study of two sharply differing temperaments and attitudes, and the resulting clash of wills rather than the tensions of the external world creates the conflicts in the narrative. Tom is at war with himself: "At bottom sincere, he is seduced by a need for success into bewildering insincerities."[14] He is at the same time contemptuous of the qualities in him which bring success in his world, and he feels envious of David's simple idealism. Yet, because David's simple nature is a rebuke to his friend's twisted personality, Tom tries to destroy what he envies in David in an effort to justify his own cynicism: "This chap has something I lack and want: a sort of pure sincerity," he admits to his sister, Cornelia. "He'll go far——and be miserable as the devil. . . . I want to give him the saving moderation. Then we could both be saved."

David, on the other hand, who is slow like Quincy Burt and who tries to find "his way through his emotions rather than his intellect,"[15] is the unborn man struggling to become a Person. Like Frank, he discovers the way through a mystical vision:

> David knew through his shut eyes, walking the world, how he was carried within a world of ceaseless substance: how he was substance within it: how his moving and knowing through Flesh was Spirit. . . . And though he knew not he had seen, there was within him . . . life of a vision.
>
> The world was a Dark Mother. The Night of the miracle of worlds was fleshed and was . . . an infinite path. . . . And he within her, moving with the world toward the movelessness of birth.

David's quest of the Spirit through Flesh involves him with women, most of whom function as foster mothers. The country girl serving as a housemaid in his uncle's home, "mothered his distress. . . . When she judged he had had enough of her, very calmly, very like a mother weaning her child, she had put him aside." His cousin Lois kisses David once but then girlishly treats him "as part of the parade" and "the Narcissus of David's love found a shrunken ego." Constance Bardale gives him sex without love and proves herself "a wonderful woman: a true American in specialization." When David protests his love for her, Constance, like his old mathematics teacher, leads him to a mirror: "He saw his face like that of a rather unknowing boy upon whom a good-hearted friend had played a delicious joke. . . . The delusion of love was rent away. . . . Tacitly he let slip all he had dreamed of woman, all he had dreamed of love." Caroline Lord, a successful business woman, invites his passion; but "she had not reached thirty years to be seduced by a boy who would not marry. . . ." Cornelia, who "would lead David the way of his dreams, the way of his young gods," leads him instead to Helen Daindrie, despite her own unrequited love for him, when Tom's machinations begin to threaten David's soul.

Thus the novel dwindles off into marriage without resolving the major theme: David's struggle to become a Person. Evidently, Frank was already thinking of this story as the first installment of David Markand's long search for self, a search which in *The Death and Birth of David Markand* (not to be published until 1934) takes him away from Helen. Consequently, the reader of *The Dark Mother*, who has been led to expect a definite resolution of the problems posed by the conflict between Tom and David, is left unsatisfied by the ending of the novel, which by its irresoluteness reduces the psychological conflict to the level of a case study.

In general, however, the technique in *The Dark Mother* is more skillful than that in *The Unwelcome Man.* The descriptions of nature are more poetic; those of the city of New York, more forceful and vivid. In such descriptive passages, Frank is primarily concerned with the effect of environment upon character, and he accordingly tries to register that effect in terms of the emotional essence of the scene rather than in the surface details:

> David was walking on Wall Street. Glass casements fronting heavy buildings, huge masonry pillared by slender stone—the grace and loom, the hypocrisy of Power. Spawn of the buildings: men with naked singing nerves like wires in storm, . . . Furious streets. . . . Streets narrow and somber that curled like smoke across his feet. Streets eaten with secret moods. Streets cluttered and twisting with pent power. . . . Streets slumberous like pythons. . . .
>
> A wide gash of sky. The sun was a stranger. The blue was a burn.

The city inspires most of the social criticism scattered through the narrative. Tom finds the "true inwardness" of New York's rising skyline in the passion for high rents, "a handy substitute for other, remoter standards." He predicts that future historians will say ". . . Money was so deep their worship that they misprized all treasures of life which did not blatantly announce it. They left their walls empty of beauty, their larders empty of health, their houses empty of grace, in order to pay high rents to the lords of land. . . . The height of New York rentals and the high buildings that were their symbols became the chief expression of Metropolitan Art! . . . Surely these were a foolish people, ripe for destruction."

As in *Our America*, the social commentary in *The Dark Mother* points toward the vague Socialist theories current in the early 1920's. Tom warns the naïve David that "one must of course despise business . . . . that it is the scramble of rather lowly-evolved and very greedy persons . . . . that the elements that lift up the Rockefellers and the Morgans and the Hills are chiefly the singlemindedness of the stupid, the unimaginative and the dishonest." Moreover, the "law is pandar to all of business's ugly lusts."

David dismisses these tirades as expressions of his friend's twisted pragmatism, but he senses some truth in Tom's criticisms when the human struggle for mere existence is pressed upon him:

> Business was indeed a scramble in life's gutters for food: . . . Production was in a state of wasteful anarchy. But men had somehow preferred to ship their fair food from the fields . . . and drop it in the filth of a million scurrying feet, . . . Here they preferred to fight for it like pigs nosing to a trough: to expend their energies and debase their spirits for its hoarding and for the depriving of others. . . . Why should the simpler way not have been found, by which all men might have what they needed to eat—expend the rest of their forces in higher works? . . .

David's uncle, Anthony Deane, personifies the American business man and the cult of success as public service. He explains proudly that the one way to earn real money in New York is "to think of absolutely nothing else: to give time to nothing else. There's the American Ideal of Service for you. . . . America is the result! . . . We've made it. . . . We're making it."

The characterization of Anthony Deane reveals Frank's increasing skill as a novelist, for Deane is more than a stereotype or a caricature. His interest in David is convincing; and he is appropriately ineffective in his home, where he is the bumbling father, dominated by his wife and manipulated by his daughters. But in his office he sheds his native shyness to become the assured, competent executive. This contrast, as Bittner observes, "makes the use of him for ironic comment on the 'practical man' all the more effective, for he is so good a businessman and so uneasy a husband, father, and host that we see he really has thought of nothing but making money."[16] Unfortunately Deane remains a minor character in the book; yet he lives as a personality while Tom and David, despite their prolonged analyses of self and each other, never come to life. The psychoanalytic method smothers them in words.

The Dark Mother is not a satisfactory novel largely because Frank has not yet devised a technique which will effectively link his temperament and his esthetics into a meaningful whole. The novel remains a collection of brightly polished parts. That Frank was aware of this deficiency is evident in his conscious experiments with form in his next four narratives, which he calls "the lyric novels."[17]

CHAPTER 3

The Lyric Novels

BY THE TIME *The Dark Mother* was published in October, 1920, Frank, spurred to intense creative work by his mystical vision, had completed a first draft of *City Block* and three parts of *Rahab*. By November he had finished *Rahab* and outlined *Holiday*. During the first two months of 1921, he again went South, this time traveling through Virginia, South Carolina, Alabama, Mississippi, and Louisiana with the Negro poet Jean Toomer. Upon his return to New York, Frank wrote the Foreword to the German edition of *Our America* and an essay, "The American Year," which appeared in the Munich *Neue Merkur* and in the *Nouvelle Revue Française*.[1] He continued to work on *Rahab* until he sailed in June for Portugal and Spain, a trip which inspired his plan for a cultural history of the latter country. While he was in Paris in September, he wrote the last two stories for *City Block* and finished *Rahab*. Upon his return to New York, he sent *Rahab* to the printers; the novel was published in March, 1922.[2]

Frank uses the term "lyric novels" to identify his new form which is, like a lyric poem, supposed to express subjective materials directly from the consciousness of the characters in dramatic episodes which function somewhat like the seemingly unrelated images in the poetry of Eliot and Pound. "The lyric novel . . . is an emotional rather than a rational experience, and unlike realistic fiction, its aesthetic does not rely on reflection of life" in a conventional narrative fashion.[3] The movement is inward in search of the inner drama of the character. There is a moment of objective activity followed by a connective interval of emotion and reflection, not logical or structured thought but the fragments and flashes of the subconscious. These unspoken monologues reveal the soul's turmoil, but there are few outward signs of this distress. Mental impressions are underscored and projected by using a poetic style featuring morbid, fevered images.

In attempting to realize this new form, Frank experiments with narrative devices like stream-of-consciousness, flashback, dreams, juxtaposed scenes, and metaphorical language—techniques which are associated with the development of the novel in the 1920's. But to his pioneering in form Frank adds his concept of the Person, the character who tries to grasp his unity with all things and to live in the Whole despite his sufferings as a small part of that Whole. "Unlike the assumptions in 'realism' that the individual is real—and immortal, so that he may be portrayed analytically, historically, linearly—the premise for Frank is that the individual is unreal and is transformed into truth instantaneously, non-linearly, *only* as the timeless and spaceless Presence speaks in him."[4] Religious symbols and psalmlike chants suggest this mystical transport. Thus, the novels become "proofs of God," which are "revealed to every human being when he has the experience of love and calls it beauty. This sense of beauty is the sense of sharing Cosmos."[5]

I *The Search*

In *Rahab* the story of Fanny Luve's struggle to find some meaning in her blighted life is told in a series of flashbacks which are interrupted by scenes from the present. The novel opens with the type of vignette which later characterizes *City Block*. A youthful Jew, Samson Brenner, calls at a house of prostitution, but the girl he seeks is out. The madam, Mrs. Luve, who has been reading in her small, black Bible, maneuvers him into sipping wine with her. Their awkward conversation is interspersed with Brenner's thoughts, which are presented in the guise of speech but identified as unspoken by the use of a long dash, such as the French use to indicate dialogue. The scene ends with some lines of verse suggestive of the young man's emotional reactions: "He felt:——I am disappearing./. . . There will be words moving in light:/There will be lighted words. . . ."[6]

Scene 2 opens with an unannounced flashback in which Fanny Dirk is seduced by Harry Luve, a wealthy, gallant young Southerner, who then insists upon a secret marriage until he finishes college. The flashback is interrupted by a brief return to the present in which Mrs. Luve, sipping her wine, thinks: "——I want you to see me!" Then her story resumes. (These alternations become less frequent as the narrative episodes of the flashbacks grow longer.)

Bored with college, Harry turns to liquor, gambling, and women. During Fanny's pregnancy he starts on a two-year skid toward the gutter, a descent which is described impressionistically:

> Face clawed close by myriad tiny fears and horrors. . . . Hands dead white leaves, dry, crackling at his sides. . . . Bodies huddled like hulks of beef or pork, covered with rags. He floats above them. . . .
>
> . . . A man, beside a barrel, let his fingers trail like grey worms through the sawdust. . . . Harry Howland Luve laboriously counted his fingers . . .——one two three four . . . : my God! where is my fifth finger? "I lack a finger! I lack a finger!" . . . He walked quiet now, looking on the pavement tracks for his lost finger.

Meanwhile, Fanny stumbles upon her first faint concept of the Person: "But I am a broken curve, a splintered part of a Circle I cannot see . . . My thought's a finger feeling from the line of my brokenness for a Roundness beyond me." When a Jewish attorney from Washington, Leon Dannenberg, arrives on the scene and recognizes her unhappiness, Fanny has an affair with him because he gives her a kind of spiritual vision of herself and the world. "You make me feel that I have roots," she says, and he tells her that "There is God." When they part, she promises to "find out what this great truth is . . this truth I know, the first truth I have ever known . . that you are holy."

Harry is saved by an evangelist and finds his redemption in describing his sinful life to college students. When he returns to his little family, proud of "the cant molds of his ideals," he sanctimoniously throws Fanny out, "*for the cause of fornication*" when she, inspired by his confessionals, tries to tell him how Leon had helped her "to push up from . . . my death under the ground" where Harry had buried her.

Rejecting suicide, Fanny heads for New York. In Washington she goes to Dannenberg's office but decides not to see him: " 'I must seek you,' she whispered . . . 'differently.' " But she envisions a meeting with him during which he urges her to be born again by letting her old self die. In New York she becomes the mistress of Christopher Johns, her first employer—information conveyed in a flashback of her story. She rejects Johns finally because she interprets her dependence upon him as a weakness, as a falling back into the destructive element of self instead of a falling "upward upon God." She protests to Johns that she will poison others as long as she seeks to be healed of her wound:

> That is what makes the world endlessly hurt the world. . . . Each human soul, wounded by another soul, seeks a soul to be healed. And the wound is passed along, endlessly, endlessly. . . . *I must not seek to be healed.* That is what I have learned. . . . We seek to be well. We crave peace . . . . love . . . . I came to you with my bloody soul . . . . and now you are bloody, too. And I no less bleeding. Do you understand just a little, Jonathan? why the peace you gave me, the care and the tenderness . . . why all that has been wrong? . . .
>
> Do you hear me, God, wherever you are? . . . I slipped back from falling. I couldn't go on falling upward upon you. Not then. I shall try again.

Harmony is not to be found in selfish compromises or in substitutions but only in becoming the Person who accepts all of life, its good and its bad, as parts of the Whole and who learns to overcome his separatistic ego.

The difficulty in achieving this mystical growth creates the dramatic tensions of the novel. After leaving Johns, Fanny slips into poverty and then delirium. Crouched over a smoking heater in a dingy room, she demands to know from God the point of suffering. With Job she cries: "What is this sense of holiness that will not leave? Which is it, God? I must know: I have sinned or I am holy?" She becomes very ill, performs a dance of death in which she claims that God has needed her, too, as part of his design: "A great Peace came. . . . Warm waters . . . washed her of doubt and of weakness, washed her at last of self." Having purged her soul of selfishness, she is ready for awareness of Wholeness. She is nursed to health by Clara, a girl whom she had known in Johns' office and who had offered her love, which she had rejected as too easy a way out. Clara and her friends, all kept women, persuade Fanny to take a house with them and to manage it.

The house is not an open brothel but a meeting place for the girls and their men: a police lieutenant named Statt, in charge of the Vice Squad; a gambling house operator named Abraham Mangel; and Clara's friend, Judge Mark Pfennig. Fanny seems to add something to the life of each one: "These wills touched hers!" In Mangel, she stirs a sense of guilt in his subconscious, which is voiced in lines of verse: "You have shown me, Luve woman, that Tessie is my daughter/. . . O if I could say that, say: Father!/Not:——a whore and a dirty Jew that keeps her."

After six years of this arrangement, Mangel, overcome by his conscience, has one of his gambling establishments raided and prepares to tell the district attorney of the collusion of the police with the gamblers. Fanny refuses to let Statt have Mangel killed in the house; but Statt warns her that, if she does not, the house will be closed by the police. Mangel is murdered in front of a cafe; Fanny and Clara, who is now seriously ill, are tossed into the street; shortly thereafter Clara dies of pneumonia in a hospital. Fanny comes back eventually to where she was at the start of the novel: the madam of a brothel sipping wine with an impatient customer whom she has been trying to reach with her story in order to learn from his reaction the Knowledge that Leon promised. If the sensitive young man now turns away from the house and his girl, it will be a sign that he has understood the spiritual wholeness of Fanny's actions, has grasped the significance of her destruction of self for others.

But Samson's eyes "died from the eyes of Fanny." He leaves the room with his arm around his girl:

> Fanny sat down where she had sat before. Beyond her rigid gaze was an empty place. Beyond the empty place was the Night. Within her gaze was the Night. Her eyes held nothing.
>
> "And a Jew," she murmured "a Jew was to bring me Light."
>
> . . . .
>
> "——and God?"
>
> Suddenly her eyes were hard. "Think of him," she spoke. . . . "Your Light-bearer, your Prophet, your Voice in the Wilderness ——there he is, out there, in the arms of Thelma . . . Fanny, dare to think."

Daring at last to think—and to see—Fanny finds "Light," but finds it within her, not without, in a moment of mystical illumination: "Then, from the wreckage of her features there was born a smile making them clear and sharp, making them fair and high. A Light shone in them."[7]

Like her biblical predecessor Rahab, a prostitute who hid the Jewish spies in the city of the Philistines, Fanny Luve has been "saved alive" after the destruction of her refuge. She has not been saved by the Jews: her refusal to betray Mangel destroyed her little world; the young Samson brings no light to her. But she has won her own salvation by recognizing that "Life is a wound that only life can heal" and by becoming thereby the

Person who knows that he belongs in the design, is a part of the Whole.

In Frank's account of his own illumination he wrote: "There must be in men's hearts a knowing whereby their frightful suffering has meaning." This knowing, he then observed, is inevitably religious since it "alone conserves in man a creative attitude toward suffering." Thus, for Frank, the characters of his fictions become the "definitions, axioms, propositions, proofs . . . . of God." Since the absolute reality of the old orders of proof are gone, he now finds the new evidence in the Fanny Luves and the "wondrously hard and real" persons of *City Block*: "All these men and women, stated, tending toward their inevitable development, toward their inevitable apocalypse of Truth, are to me quite in the same relation that his logical and Euclidean formulae and laws must have held for Spinoza." The significant difference is that Frank, "the ship-wrecked modern," must first create new myths, histories, axioms, and laws in order to establish his "proofs of God." He describes the way in Notebook VII:

> The process is mysterious. . . . There is then, for me, some relationship between my full living and the process, to which I am condemned by the deliquescence of my age, to CREATE MY OWN SUBSTANCES . . . FOR THE ERECTION OF MY DIVINE DESIGN. . . . When life becomes inevitable to me, I merely accept it: and having accepted it, I proceed to make it over into the stuffs of my work. . . . We behold, in our straitened mind-cell, separate strands of the Whole. And we attempt to bring these strands together within the moment of our consciousness. But they reach forth into dimensions vastly beyond us: where indeed they conjoin into a unitary resolution. It is futile to try to force them into their almighty unity, within our petty fragment of a mind: and it is futile to deplore our failure. Better to watch, in the very insoluble apartness of the strands of Life within our minds, a gorgeous proof of how vastly Life looms beyond us.[8]

This statement is not only an accurate rationale of all Frank's novels but an especially useful one as a key to the method and meaning of the "lyric novels," which are the creations of Frank's mystical illumination.

II *Unanimism in White*

Although *City Block* had a long period of gestation—Frank sketched the general plan and some notes for individual stories as early as 1916—the published book is not just a collection of the stories written from these early notes. Eleven of the fourteen narratives were written after Frank's revelation, and the remaining three were revised or wholly rewritten versions of previously drafted or published tales.[9]

The early versions of these stories are simple fictions in the vein of Frank's first two novels. They, like the sketches in the notebook for 1916, dramatize the ironic futility of life in a modern city. But the stories as they appear in *City Block* reflect the change in point of view attributable to Frank's mystic vision. Instead of futility, the characters dramatize the kind of spiritual triumph seen in Fanny Luve and expressed in Frank's description of the process of discovering proofs of God. The characters, however, are seldom aware of the triumph. They remain lonely, bewildered, suffering souls who are battered by the impersonal blows of life; but something has happened to them—"the process is mysterious"—which is at once "gorgeous proof of how vastly Life looms beyond us" and of the mystic reality of the Whole.

The stories are supposed to represent parts of that Whole, to reveal in their increasing complexity a kind of progressive awareness of the mystical union of all. Frank in a prefatory note "assures the reader that *City Block* is a single organism and that its parts should be read in order."[10] As in Anderson's *Winesburg, Ohio*, which Frank had publicized in the *Seven Arts*, the individual narratives are related in *City Block*; but there is no central character like George Willard to act as a unifying agent. Instead, Frank tries to establish connectives by having the major characters in one story take minor roles in another, a technique also used by Anderson in *Winesburg, Ohio*. The Lanichs and the Rabinowichs, for example, appear in each other's stories but have no important part in them. Esther Lanich, for whom "time is a barren field with no horizon," feels superior to warm, gentle Lotte Rabinowich, whose moronic son fondles little Flora, Esther's unwanted child. Esther also feels superior to Sophie Breddan, whose story is a tragic one of frustrated desire for a child that stands in ironic contrast to Esther's hatred of her daughter and to her determination not to have any more children.

Fanny Luve turns up in two of the narratives, although she has no story of her own in the book since the one Frank had sketched for her in his notebook was discarded when it grew into *Rahab*. In "Accolade," an interesting modern version of O. Henry's famous "Gift of the Magi," Fanny takes the drunken, defeated Clarence Lipper to her shabby room; drinks with him "to the common Nothing we are and we share"; but gives him, when she learns that he has squandered on drink the money that he had intended to spend on ivory combs for his wife's Christmas present, the silver hair brushes that she had received from her husband twenty years before and never used. They are her accolade, her gift, "fresh and clean," like Lipper's wife and the girl Fanny had been. In "Faith," Fanny forces a love-starved pair, a lonely English nurse and a married policeman, to stop trying to cram their hopeless love into a back bedroom and to have faith in their separate worlds.

Aimee Lipper, in search of a Christmas gift for her husband, turns up in one of the more complex stories in the latter part of the book. "Ecclesia Sanctae Teresae" reveals Frank's characteristic amalgamation of Naturalism and mysticism in his presentation of sex and religion, a coupling which disturbs, if it does not shock, the orthodox and is usually more confusing than enlightening. In this story a virile young priest, Father Luis Dennis, is tormented by his desire to discover the secret of life which the hurrying crowds on Christmas Eve seem to possess:"——They who are naught and who think naught are in the secret. I who think, am outside." Evidently, thought rather than emotion has made him a priest; his mother had wanted him to become rich—"In this country, when you're not rich there's no use"—and he had thwarted her will by his choice of vocations. Now he is beset with religious doubts. Awaiting him outside his room above the church is Mr. Kandro, a shadowy figure from Sophie Breddan's story, "Murder." Like the priest, Mr. Kandro is consumed with desire. In his lonely sixty-five years he has never had sexual intercourse and now that he believes that he never will he wants to know what a priest does when desire seizes him: "A woman's body . . . . is a healing we can take whole upon us. . . . Is it Pride and the love of your Hurt that keeps you also away from the white healing?"

Mr. Kandro slips away, and Aimee Lipper glides into the priest's room. Troubled by some vague feeling of sexual inadequacy in herself as a loving wife, she seeks a gift for her husband so that she may become a giver in love instead of just a receiver. Standing close before the priest, she becomes for him the "white straight healing" as he tells himself, "What is Sin but a lack, a great Hunger?" They have intercourse; and, as she departs gratefully to tell Clarence, "a woman wise and sure of herself," she says joyously, "I have something now to give at last to my husband!"

Father Dennis too feels exultant. His spirit dances: "danced upon the Past, . . . danced upon the Future. . . . The world swung . . . Jerusalem packed with prayer, Rome red with argument." As the sense of the flesh fades, he struggles to retain it: "O splendor of your flesh, come let me know you, though Sin must come along." Then he thinks of his "blessed saviour Church!" which will give flesh and sin to him and, "like a frightened boy, he rushed praying down stairs. . . ."

This ambiguous conclusion indicates that the story is meant to be more than a sordid tale of sexual frustrations and priestly infidelities. Bittner thinks that it is meant to be "an attack on the confusion between puritanism and purity," which carries the implication that denial of sex is the sin.[11] The way to things of the spirit is through the things of this world, not through rejection of them. Life is the healing agent. Both Father Dennis and Aimee Lipper seek a reality which the church tries to ignore, the reality which it equates with sin. Their act is morally wrong and Frank's prose, especially in such banal exclamations as Aimee's—"I have something now to give at last to my husband!" —fails to place her objective in the proper perspective. Frank intends the sexual actions to be symbolic experiences of the spirit, as well as the flesh; but his Naturalistic handling of them obscures rather than illumines, and these symbols and their religious meaning remain obscure. The characters have supposedly found redemption in the flesh because their motives are pure: they are trying to find and develop their spiritual natures, to find a new kind of faith to replace the loss of the old God. And in *City Block* the only hopeless failures are those characters who are spiritually dead or indifferent. A difficulty arises, however, when Frank tries to make the word flesh.

Although "Ecclesia Sanctae Teresae" was the last story written for the book, the concluding tale, composed in Paris in September, 1921, is paradoxically entitled "Beginning." Kloucek perceptively reasons that this story "is a prologue appearing as epilogue for the very reason that the novel's central theme is a vision which is never explicitly stated but which must grow in the reader's own consciousness—the vision of the mystic unity of life, the feeling that all life arises from Desire—and a prologue carrying a statement of this theme can be better understood by a reader at the end rather than at the beginning."[12]

"Beginning" is the story of Paolo Benati, the fifteen-year-old son of Italian immigrants who operate a barbershop in the Block. Working at his bootblack's stand, Paolo senses the longings of his customers and the passersby as he watches them "trailing each a little verdant banner" and sees "these banners catch upon each other, intertwine, draw close the face of a man and the face of a woman." He asks the "question of the Night" that everyone must ask: "what are you? what do you feel?" The question is a "silver whisper . . . . a whisper against stillness, silver against black." He feels that the question is wrong, but that it must be asked: "It was life. All life a whisper or a shriek . . silver or red . . against the silent black."

Having heard the stories of the men and women, having felt "the rent of pain that was each voice of their hearts, each word of their minds against Night . . . . a rent . . against immobile fate," Paolo yearns subconsciously "—To bring them stillness, to bring them whiteness." His experience becomes a suggestion of the Whole that Frank would have each achieve through the development of a mystical spiritual awareness of unity beyond the disparate, usually clashing, fragments of existence. Paolo says:

> I did not seek the discording questions that made clear the night and the stirring fleck of myself. I was enwrapped in heat and darkness beyond will. Then the birth came: the subtle thread of my being, of the beings of them whom I crossed in the Block, . . . the pity of their whisper or their shriek . . the silver or the blood . . against immobile stillness.
>
> I have thought no farther than this. Again and again: "to bring the stillness they break, the whiteness they mar" . . the words came and were attuned—these words—with my night. For white and black, I have found since, are one.

Paolo's suicide is also a beginning in the sense that death is not an ending; other lives will appear to ask the same questions that Paolo asked and to struggle for Wholeness. Paolo has given his stories "to the man that wrote them," each story being an expression of his question and a fragment of the Wholeness of *City Block*. The author had not believed in the stories until he, too, had suffered great anguish of spirit and had cried, "I have no claim on other than my fate. So be it . . . There is no injustice . . . there is God." Then the dead Paolo had seized him and made him the instrument of his vision. Or thus did Frank's mystical experience inspire the dormant sketches for stories in his notebooks by giving them an organic unity which would justify his considering his collection one of his "lyric novels."

In his attempt to present sexuality as a sacrament in some of the more complex stories in *City Block*, Frank was not attacking religion but its dogmas. He realized, however, that his Naturalistic treatment of sex might invite censorship by the Puritan remnant resurgent in the 1920's. Since John Sumner, of the New York Society for the Prevention of Vice, was crusading for book "purity" when *City Block* was ready for the press, Frank published the novel himself in September, 1922, in a limited edition of 1,250 copies. Actually Boni and Liveright were the publishers, but Frank gave his name to the copyright so that any action by Sumner would have to be brought against him instead of the publishing house. Sumner did not act, but the first trade edition of the book did not appear until 1929, after the purity movement had subsided and Scribner's had become Frank's publishers.

III *Unanimism in Black*

While preparing *City Block* for the printers, Frank sketched in Notebook VII "a magnificent theme" for a novel about the deep South, which he tentatively titled, "Carnival":

> A study of life in a small Mississippi or Georgia town—the dearth of outlet, the constant, terrible petty repressiveness, the falsity of the preaching, the cheat of the "movies"—the gradual growth of the hidden passionate Tumor—and its inevitable outbreak in 1) the Negro's raping a girl and 2) the whole community's lynching of the negroes. Holiday. Festival. Carnival.
>
> *Juxtaposed*: the ugly huddled "white" town of frame houses, tin-front banks . . . and the *Niggertown* hinterland of sparse pine . . . and paintless shanties.

On the opposite page of the notebook is the opening paragraph of the novel, which emphasizes the music of the Negroes and the inability of the whites to hear it or to create any like it.

In September, after the appearance of *City Block*, Frank took a short trip into the Black Belt with Negro poet Jean Toomer, who coached him in the nuances of Negro dialect. Frank had been in the South before, had made a speech at the Tuskegee Institute, and had met George Washington Carver at the school.[13] Now, traveling with Toomer, he posed as a Negro in order to avoid incidents while he tried to feel with these exiles from American civilization. He rode in Jim Crow coaches, lived with Toomer's friends, spoke in a Negro church on science and religion, only to learn later that his audience had not understood the meaning of the word *science.* He found his theme in the mutual resentment in the two races: the whites resent that the black can sing and laugh and appear happy; the blacks laugh to cover their hatred, and they practice Christian charity as an act of self-preservation against their self-destroying hatred. Their music and dance are a means of surviving in a hostile world. Stirred by his emotional reaction to his experience, Frank returned to Darien, Connecticut, and wrote the first draft of his new novel in a month. Revisions were finished by March, 1923; and *Holiday* was published in August.

The details in the narrative are those of the notebook sketch, except for the elimination of "the cheat of the 'movies'" and the deliberately ambiguous treatment of the rape. The town of Nazareth, somewhere on the Gulf of Mexico, is shoddy, brittle, repressed: "Nazareth moving down is apart from the world. . . . And within, flecking the world's rapt sweep, the houses like splinters, the faces like dry flakes, jagged thoughts, pressed emotions."[14] Its longing for the City across the bay is symbolized in its rickety, rotting pier: "The pier is the cluttering broken wooden will of the town, thrust out . . . into the bay of the world."

The tramp steamer *Psyche* arrives at the patched-up wharf. As the ship swings in alongside, "a negro slips on the greasy, narrow deck," falls into the water, and drowns as white Nazareth watches. Bob Hade, the town's best swimmer, refuses to wet his white flannel pants since there are "'Plenty o' niggers round.'" The incident drifts into the consciousness of the inhabitants of Niggertown, but it is no cause for action since it is just one more episode in the old mindless conflict of races. Furthermore, Frank is not interested in the usual melodramatic expression of that conflict but in a more subtle theme, one related to his concept of Wholeness in which man's cruelty to man is merely an extension of his separatistic ego. He explains the point in a comment published three months after the novel appeared:

> *Holiday* is a story as simple and as direct as I could make it, of one of the greatest of American dramas: the struggle in the South between the white race and the black. To the artist there is no right and no wrong in this drama: there is only beauty, only truth, only life. The truths of the white race are pitted in merciless conflict against the truths of the negro. From this meeting of fundamental forces there arises a tragedy which has haunted me long. . . .

> There are no villains in *Holiday*, no heroes. The two protagonists are White Town and Black Town; the white girl, Virginia, and the black man, John, are significant in so far as forces, hungers, passions, and ideals vastly greater than themselves run through them and grow articulate in their deeds. For here is a dual world, each part of which yearns in its racial way for self-expression, for joy, for life, for God; each part of which *profoundly loves and needs what the other part possesses*, and through the fateful circumstances of American life, all this energy of desire is locked into opposition and distrust so that it becomes channelled not in some fair communion but in an orgy of blood and horror. This ironic state is tragedy, surely, but tragedy quite as profound for the white oppressors and lynchers (victims of their own hate and love) as for their negro victims.[15]

Virginia Hade, weary of the whiteness which stifles her and makes her men folks brittle or empty, envies the Negroes. Her father reproves her for staring wistfully at Negro girls "with low-cut open waists, singing and picking fruit," in the same hungry way that John Cloud, the Negro, watches her. Her retort is an angry challenge to her father: "What are you men afraid of? . . . The darkies love their place. They're a lot happier and better off, I sometimes think, in their place than we in ours. . . . It's you, with your fanatical obsessions——" But her counterpart, John Cloud, is also consumed by his desire for some warmth in human relations: "Cold white world——I'll make you warm——that'll warm me!" The cowed, passive Negroes urge him to adopt the black's conventional mask; an old mammy warns, "Ah sees de white look in yo' nigger eyes!" and then she adds, while "spittin' in de face ob all" the skulking Nigger preachers, that the Lord is black and he hates "de white look. . . ."

John walks through the woods to the beach and plunges naked into the cooling water. Virginia, spurning the heat of the revival tent, wanders to a spot overlooking the beach where John has left his clothes. When he returns for them and stands over her, naked, they are drawn toward each other by desire; but the color barrier keeps them apart. John quickly dresses, and they talk haltingly, both struggling with their prejudices. He takes out a knife and begins to whittle a stick. She pulls a small knife from her stocking and offers to swap. He examines the knives and says, " 'Taint a fair bargain, . . . Not for you, and not for me. . . ." She insists, however, upon an exchange. He clasps her hand, and they rise, their bodies close; but in his subconscious looms the fact, "*——I am John Cloud. Nigger.*" Her face becomes unreal before him, and he turns to go.

In this way Frank makes their intercourse merely symbolic and also suggests the superiority of John. Virginia's emotion-charged thoughts, expressed in verse, spell out the turmoil of her being, which is torn between two worlds. She cuts herself at the waist, an act symbolic of her conscious determination to break the pull of the black world and of her unconscious use of the knife as a sexual organ. The action is also a betrayal of John, for this symbolic cut with his knife, instead of rape or anything that she says, provokes his lynching.

As Virginia returns to Main Street, the crowd drifts from the revival tent. It is smoldering in a half-roused state of emotion. The meeting has been an unsuccessful one; God has proved "hard to git holt on." The dry rasping voice of the preacher "ain't h'isted" them up or out of themselves: "It is tumescence cheated. In the mass threatened with dispersal lives still the glow that should have come to flame." So the failure of religion contributes directly to the racial conflict. For the crowd turns to the preparations for a lynching with calm gladness; the people are willing servants of emotions that they understand. They no longer throb with frustration in the unconsummated act of religious passion; they have found release for the wealth of their substance, and in Bob Hade they have found a tangible God Head, who will "h'ist" them up. Ignoring his sister's repeated protests that she is unharmed, Hade simply points out to the mob that the knife Virginia carries belongs to John Cloud: "He does not lift his voice. He does not urge. His words are free. They have wings. They have faith. They bear with them a glamorous life all dawning."

The "little sleek plump" preacher offers a half-hearted protest: "What are those guns for, brothers? You have just come from Christ." The women draw him to them as he resignedly mutters: "I have done my duty." The benches are dragged "from the Tent of God" to the Square, where "they have become these smiling open rows" around a solitary cottonwood. "The crowd takes seats. . . . It has a bloom of peace" as "Nazareth waits in a mute gay dance. . . . The tree, with its nude branch, stands and points up waiting.——*Upon the black branch of the black tree let there be Fruit!/Let there be seed, let there be fruit for my passion!*"

The armed mob tramps through Niggertown, which appears deserted. It finds John, who has refused to run, with his fianceé, Mary, and his mother, who is kneeling before him. The "man rope twisting" is weakened for a moment by the tableau; it "threatens to make them men with eyes to see this quiet straight man and his molten women." But Bob Hade contemptuously asks John if he expects the women to save him, and "The crisis is behind him of the Rope that almost turned to man and youth and man."

Virginia lies in her bed, listening to the murmur of the crowd, wondering if she will stop the murder. The murmur becomes a howl as the mob finds release for its pent passion in the hanging and burning of a black Christ. White Nazareth spends its lust; Virginia sleeps, soothed by the silence; and "The *Psyche* stands at the empty pier that points from Nazareth out into the world."

Holiday is at once the most lyrical of the "lyric novels" and the best illustration of the experimental techniques Frank uses in these impressionistic tales. Since the theme is the tragedy of the group in a dual world, rather than that of the individual, and since the emphasis is upon mood and atmosphere, Frank's use of verse is not so intrusive or artificial as in *Rahab*. Similarly the articulation of subconscious and unconscious thought is more natural and appropriate in this novel. Such thoughts are minor melodies in a symphony of the South, whose major theme is the tragedy of that land.

But, while Frank's use of the unanimist concept of the group as the focal character of a novel makes many of his narrative devices effective, it is also the source of the major weakness in *Holiday*: characterization.[16] The characters are either stereotypes or abstractions; not even John Cloud or Virginia Hade registers as personalities. Their meeting is casual; their conflict merely symbolic; the lynching is almost impersonal. As Frank says, "The two protagonists are White Town and Black Town." Virginia and John are little more than abstractions of the conflict; they are dreamy, even unconscious in their actions. The reader misses the dramatic impact of personalities. The symbolism of black and white carries the theme adequately, but the consequent depersonalization of personae raises a doubt as to the effectiveness of this fictional technique and suggests why the "lyric novels" fail to satisfy most readers. With *Chalk Face* Frank ended his experiments with the form and did not publish any fiction for almost a decade.

IV *Critical Broadsides*

In the spring of 1923 Frank sketched a mystery story—*The Other Room*—in Notebook VIII. By June 18, only two months after the final revision of *Holiday*, he had completed a rough draft of the new story and given it the tentative title *Who Is a Man*. But for the rest of the year he was too busy with other projects to work on the novel. He wrote some articles for various little magazines and a new preface for a second edition of *The Unwelcome Man*; he made a translation of Romains' *Lucienne*. In September, he decided to live apart from his wife and moved from Connecticut to Manhattan, where he started preparing a collection of his essays for publication and planning another trip to Spain.

He arrived in Paris early in November and was subjected to "dismal lionizing & painful gaiety" until Christmas. His books had made him famous in the city of letters; he was received with acclaim at Shakespeare and Company, where he and James Joyce exchanged inscribed copies of *Ulysses* and *City Block*.[17] On December 27, Frank headed for Madrid, traveling by way of Avignon, Marseilles, Algiers, Bou-Saada, Morocco, and Seville. During a month at Bou-Saada, while studying Moorish life, he corrected and typed the rough draft of the mystery novel, now entitled *To Life*. He reached Madrid on February 22, 1924, and plunged into hard work on the book on Spain, recasting the plan for it conceived back in June, 1921. In March, a collection of his essays was published by Boni and Liveright under the title *Salvos*.[18]

Most of the twenty-one essays in *Salvos* had previously appeared in magazines during the years 1916-1924; they were reprinted, except "For a Declaration of War" (first published in 1924), in chronological order without changes in the texts but with brief "postcripts" for some of the pieces. In these additions, Frank updates his opinions, apologizes for unkindnesses or inadequacies in the original, or, in a few instances, enlarges on his first observations. The subtitle of the volume claims that it is "An Informal Book about Books and Plays," which covers all of the selections accurately except for a portrait of Charlie Chaplin and "A Thought on Photography."

In these occasional pieces Frank is usually an interesting and often a challenging critic. His perceptions are original if somewhat bumptious in the manner of young critics in the 1920's. With equal zest he pricks with his rapier "the myth of Shakespeare"—a product of the bard's charm instead of his profundity—or takes the broad axe to Joyce Kilmer's *Literature in the Making*: "In any less supine society, would not Mr. Joyce Kilmer be laughed into the limbo where his dogmatic ignorance consigns him?" Frank's prose style, often obscure or turgid in his fiction, is succinct and pithy in his criticism: Booth Tarkington "is American in the way that a eunuch is chaste: as the consequence of a very deliberate and radical excision." "Main Street" is the "lyrical assault of a hurt romantic mind, by means of sharp photographic portrayal, upon the callow undifferentiated American mass." "Genius is that which grows great in narrowness: which makes a word of the mysterious Silence."

As in all of his writing Frank is concerned primarily in his criticism with "the mysterious Silence." The part must be identified with the Whole: "criticism is more than smiles and grimaces and frowns. . . . There can be no criticism for our modern world until there is a modern philosophical synthesis." Thus, there are in these early essays, as in the early books, scattered intimations of Frank's esthetic which anticipate the philosophical formulations of it to come. For example, in the essay "Vicarious Fiction," while he is attacking the crushing materialism of American life and its impact on art, he also calls for "vision." Man can be the culmination of the blind life that spews him up only when he has *felt* that life, when he has fused it into his consciousness: "Only in so far as he feels infinitude within himself is he a master. . . . And one of the ways of his effort is religion; and the other way is art." Therefore, "America needs, above all things, spiritual adventure," the achievement of "that mastering consciousness which alone can make man greater than the parts of his existence." The vision and the adventure will not be found in Realism or in Naturalism, which limit observation to the surface reality. The real is deeper, more illusive, and yields its meaning only to the mystic. So in praising Jules Romains' art, Frank sees the Frenchman, like himself, as a mystic and disciple of Spinoza: "By which I mean in brief that his materials, his characters, the emotions of his characters, are essentially treated as attributes of the Divine, as modifications containing the substance and partaking of the dynamic of the Absolute." It follows that the function of art is to bring God into life, and "the great work of art invests the individual with the ecstasy of participation in the Whole."

The implications of this view for a viable criticism and for Frank's general philosophical position are sketched in "For a Declaration of War." Starting from the two premises that "the imperative of a culture is unity" and "Culture implies a Whole," Frank claims for "the Western world a common culture: a common Whole," whose matrix is a group of spiritual and intellectual convictions within which the priest and the artist at one time worked. Since the Renaissance, however, the scientists and philosophers have destroyed on the intellectual plane all these basic convictions except the first, "the categorical imperative of any culture": "Unity is truth. This is a universe, not a multiverse." But man has temporarily lost even the power of support for this crucial assumption; hence he suffers anguish, misery, chaos: "We are in misery because we have lost the control which comes with the experience of unity and wholeness. We are in misery because we are in chaos. We live in fragmentary thoughts, desires, acts. Quite literally, the *form* of our life is decomposing. And that means death."

The war, then, is the eternal one between a cultural breakup and a cultural synthesis, the former stated philosophically in Positivism, which denies mystery in the quest for truth, and is proved negatively in positive science. If cultural synthesis is to be achieved, Art must be the instrument since it alone can bring "*into* the consciousness of mind quantities and values of life which mind alone is unable to perceive or control. . . . Art is the language which expresses vision of being that has not yet been conventionalized into simple words and concepts." It then becomes the function of criticism to naturalize "into the domain of the intellect" the forms of art so that they may become a cultural experience. And it "can perform this function only when it contacts the work of art on a common plane of spiritual and philosophical vision."

"For a Declaration of War" is significant as an embryonic statement of the main tenets of Frank's critical philosophy; but it is also one of the milestones in his evolution as a critic and an artist since it clearly reveals his recognition that the values of art and religion depend ultimately for their fruition upon the social condition. In the "lyric novels" social criticism is merely implicit in the expression of Frank's mystic vision. In this essay and in the next novel, *Chalk Face*, Frank moves into the world in search of moral applications for his concept of the Whole.

V *The Rampant Will*

In a dedicatory letter offering *Chalk Face* to his father, who supposedly shared his son's interest in mystery stories, Frank admits that the tale may seem as much a parable as a mystery; but there is for him no difference in the two forms: "What more lurid than the depths of desire, what more mysterious than the hinterlands of conscience? And what event is so great a mystery as life itself? I believe that every tale should be a mystery. . . ."[19] This point of view may be valid philosophically, but it does not lend itself readily to literary usage. The failure of this novel may be attributable, therefore, to Frank's inability to see any distinction between a mystery story and a parable.

The tale opens conventionally with the protagonist, John Mark, a brilliant young scientist, explaining that he is writing this record of his "terrible adventure" in an effort "to escape (for brief and precious hours) from this eternal Twilight" and to bring back the sense of wholeness that he has lost in his willful pursuit of Truth beyond "the innocent world of men." In telling his story, however, he lays bare the mysterious workings of the mind of a schizophrenic.

John has worked hard for his degree. For three years he has studied in the famous schools of Europe and Russia before taking a low-paying position at an institute in New York where he can carry out his research. He lives frugally, although his parents are wealthy, spending money only on rare books in which "mediaeval mystics had imposed their swelling dreams upon the flat clarities of Rome"; limiting his friendships; rejecting women altogether, though he knows himself to be "a sociable and a sensual man." But he is "less drawn by the sweet flesh than repelled by the dullness and unchastity of women." Then he falls in love with Mildred, the beautiful daughter of a very wealthy man; in her he senses a spiritual chastity of sheer sensuousness in contrast to what he considers a moralistic, possessive, pseudo-chastity in women of the world. He feels that her beauty will equate his truth; with her, he will "achieve a knowledge and a power, like [her] own beauty's wisdom beyond words."

There is, however, a serious obstacle in the path of his desire: he will need money to support a wife who is accustomed to wealth while he continues his research work. So he asks his parents for financial assistance; they refuse to give it, although his father does offer him five thousand dollars in cash to use until John can support himself "like every other married man." John does not debate the decision, but he bitterly reflects that his parents have never used their minds while he has been "able wholly, passionately, greatly, to give all"—his mind and his energy—"to the white flame of intellectual creation." Now he makes a vow to himself that he will not let the flame die from lack of nourishment. The arrogance of his determination suggests the lurking insanity in his personality; he dramatically says to himself, "The gross man is nourished with gross food: the indifferent man with any food at all. My high work called for high fuel. Not for a drudge, nor for a harried woman, nor a pretty one, nor for promiscuous pleasures. For Mildred! the essential Mildred! Nothing less."

As he walks toward Mildred's home, he finds himself mysteriously seeing with remarkable clarity the life of the city; the thought of Mildred releases him to the "bewildering freedom" of the visionary:

> I can fly where I will, and enter where I want. I see myriad women's arms, . . . I see streaming men and children and women. Each is crouched close to another. They do not see how they are streaming, streaming. They think of themselves as fixed, all else as moving.
>
> But I am moving. Something in me is fixed, and something in me is moving! . . .

Immediately he finds himself in a pleasant room, a richly furnished library, in which a handsome man, regal and relaxed, lifts his eyes as if to a visitor; but then the man throws his hands above his head as a knife enters his chest. The vision ends; John smiles at his fantasy and enters Mildred's door.

From Mildred he learns of another obstacle to his design, a rival. It seems that she likes both suitors, will live with either as a kind of test; but she is too unsure of her emotions to accept either in marriage. While explaining her attitude to Mark, she impulsively decides to summon the unidentified rival to join them, so that she can know her own mind by seeing both men together. At this point her father informs her that Philip LaMotte has been murdered; John thus learns his rival's name.

Next day John sees in the papers that the police have arrested LaMotte's serving man and are confident that the case is solved, although the man protests his innocence. But a simple-minded Negro doorboy insists that he took a stranger to LaMotte's apartment the night of the murder, a man dressed entirely in black but with a chalk-white head. The police dismiss this testimony; John visits the apartment, examines the body, and finds a scribbled note on the dead man's engagement pad indicating a planned meeting with Mildred.

John returns to his work, but he is interrupted by Doctor Isaac Stein, a great biochemist whom John admires. Their conversation reveals some of the abstract themes of the mystery. Stein comments on the seeming duality of John's mind, one part completely engaged by his work, the other part subject to speculation and "rhapsody." The latter part, he observes, is not yet in solution—not at the point yet of true condensation: "When you're wholly crystallized, Mark, then you'll be *whole!*" John objects that Stein's faith in wholeness is a mystical, highly arbitrary assumption, a convenient legacy from the Greeks and Hebrews which has been made into a working premise for human action through an act of will. But the act does not prove that the human will is unitary but blindly arbitrary; for the will can act at variance with life, thereby creating failure and anguish. This split in John Mark between will and intellect in Kloucek's view "represents the acceptance by the modern world of Cartesian dualism, of a dichotomy of body and mind that creates havoc for modern man. . . ."[20]

Mark's will, projected in a black figure with a chalk-white head, creates more havoc. The mysterious figure is seen near the car in which Mark's parents are killed when a wheel comes off as a result of someone's tampering with the wheel bolts. In a dream Mark finds himself in an isolated house high on a dark mountain. He is in a room with his parents, Mildred, LaMotte, Stein, and Mildred's father, waiting for a "sign of dawn at midnight." A ghostly white shape floats up the mountain side and through a window of another room in the house. Mark goes to the room and tries to confront the apparition. Unsuccessful, he returns to his associates, but they all now shrink from him in terror. He awakes to his shrieks in his bedroom.

It is dawn and he goes into the street where he finds the black-white figure of his will awaiting him. They cross a river on a ferry and arrive at a limekiln where the white head bids John jump into the slime of the pit and "join the white one who is you, in the other room." John's intellect seizes his will, and he leaps over the kiln to safety but twists his ankle on the rocks. Back in his room, he tries to dismiss the episode as another dream, but he cannot ignore his badly bruised ankle. Then he picks up his morning paper and reads of his parents' death in an automobile accident; he cries out, "——Oh, there must be a truth to salvage me from chaos. Life is a whirlwind? Let the Lord which is Truth speak to me then from His whirlwind." (One of the working titles for the story was *The Whirlwind*, and the Job theme is also suggested in the epigraph: "Then the Lord Answered Job Out of the Whirlwind . .")

For three weeks "of travail and unceasing night," John lies alone in his room, his life passing before him in a kind of dream or vision, all the events of his mind and heart rising like clouds around him on "the topmost peak of a mountain solitude" to which he has been lifted. He concludes that, if he is to live, he must destroy "this sin of using Truth" for his own life: "I must make my life into a facet of the Truth . . . . all these broken surfaces of being which men call bodies, things, will throb with the divinity of wholeness. The common deed of spheres beyond man's flat domain is Miracle. And it must enter now into my life."

When John confesses to Mildred, he pleads that he has done these terrible things because his will had acted ruthlessly in its pursuit of Truth and then of Beauty as personified in her: "I was ruthless, because I was in love with Beauty. I have used truth . . . as it was revealed to me, vastly beyond our miserable sphere." He begs her to save him now that he has learned "Man cannot live with Truth." But she turns away from him in fear and bewilderment, leaving him to seek his salvation alone.

In an Epilogue addressed to the reader, John (now Waldo Frank?) explains that the telling of the tale has served its primary purpose of enabling him to live among men. He recalls an evening earlier in his life in the peaceful Berkshire Hills when he was happily watching the birds in the "singing dusk." Suddenly the veil lifted and he saw nature "red in tooth and claw." A brown thrasher screeched in fear and pecked at a robber owl; robins devoured worms; "a handsome woodpecker massacred woodslugs . . . ." Every creature "in that gentle dusk . . . was engaged in bitter desperate war. . . . All the world was murdering or murdered."

Yet he decides that the world is not less fair for that, and he advises the reader who must find a moral in his story that it is in his discovery that he now greedily relives those hours and days of seeming anguish and failure, "since they were living days," days in which his heart beat highest, passion coursed most free, and he was most alive: "Out of the ash that you call history, rises the eternal flame of Love. Warm yourselves there, my brothers and my sisters. For the time will come when you will watch Love's distant gleam, desperate and nostalgic like a winter moth which beats on the frosted window trying to get in where the light burns, which beats and beats until it falls emaciate in the snow . . . ."

The manuscript of *To Life*, Frank's title for the novel, was not received with any enthusiasm by Boni and Liveright, who were already discouraged by the poor sale of *Salvos*. On March 21, Liveright sent Frank a blunt cable: "UNANIMOUSLY FEEL SHOULD NOT PUBLISH TO LIFE WHICH FIVE OF US HAVE READ STOP WOULD NOT SELL AND WOULD HURT YOU."[21] After Liveright himself read the manuscript, however, he suggested that the book be rewritten to make it clearer and that the title be changed to *Chalk Face*. Frank objected strenuously to the change in title, and he was too busy writing about Spain to bother with revisions. He made, therefore, only a few trifling changes in the manuscript, but he surrendered on the title issue. *Chalk Face* was published in October, 1924.

Frank claims that he abandoned lyrical fiction with *Chalk Face* because the vein ran out, but the real reasons seem to be that he was losing interest in the form at the same time that he was becoming increasingly preoccupied with cultural history. The loss in interest is suggested by the fact that *Chalk Face* is the least lyrical of the four novels and also the least experimental. The personifying of the subconscious will in the black-white figure contributes to the artificial atmosphere of a ghost story, but the sustaining interest of this type of fiction is lost when the duality of John Mark is revealed early in the plot, when mystery becomes allegory, and when the characters become bloodless abstractions. The technique of expressionism, which is effective for the portrayal of the feelings of the relatively emotional characters in the other lyric novels, is not satisfactory for the expression of philosophical ideas, such as the conflict in the modern world between will and intellect in *Chalk Face*. But it is adequate for the projection of a split personality and for the creation of a few striking scenes, such as the dream-fantasy of the white figure in the "other" room and the leap for life at the lime-kiln.

The major flaws in the novel seem to develop from Frank's melding of mystery and parable. Like John Mark, the author becomes the victim of his split personality: Frank does not decide whether he is writing a ghost story or a novel of ideas, a mystery or an allegory; and the resulting hybrid is a failure, for the Truth remains as enigmatic as in the Book of Job.

Most readers and commentators find the lyric novels interesting as experiments but baffling as narratives. Even a sympathetic critic, like Harlan Hatcher, has to admit that "the striving for significance and profound poetic meanings often makes the act of reading difficult. . . ." But for him "the retrospect is always definite and pleasing," and he sees in these novels a definite contribution by Frank to fiction: "He has grappled sincerely with the problem of the novel turned inward, extending its bounds. He has elevated the discussion of sex and the emotions surrounding it. He has reasserted the importance of a fervid spirituality in a material-minded age. He has evolved an impressionistic technique capable of expressing these new facets of experience. He accomplished these things at the beginning of the great tide of fiction which made use of his experiments."[22] Many more successful novelists have contributed less; and, if Frank had not at this time turned away from the writing of fiction, his story might have been different. His latter novels utilized his experiments within much enlarged dimensions of social and political concern; he, in his return to fiction, built upon what he had already created; but he had lost by that time whatever potential audience he once may have had.

CHAPTER 4

The Drama of Spain

FRANK did not consciously abandon the writing of fiction. While he was working on *Holiday* he had jotted in his note-book the idea for "Men and Dreams volumes," starting with a sequel to *The Dark Mother* to be called *The Way of Mary*, which would gather David and Tom, "these two children of *The Dark Mother* together once more . . . . in to the Heart of things." But there was a renewed compulsion in him, intensified by his work on the book about Spain, to write cultural studies, which gradually pushed fiction into the background. The notebooks also record the "tremendous flood of creating" of non-fiction following the completion of *Chalk Face*.

Frank returned to New York in September, 1924, with *The Tragedy of Spain*, as he then titled it, almost complete. On December 19, he marked the end of a phase of his career by writing in Notebook VIII this sentence: "The 'Person' is born: though still he be very young." By June, 1925, he noted that he had written 210,000 words since the previous March of which some fifty thousand went into sixty-nine articles and two plays. Among the articles are some of the twenty-five profiles appearing in the *New Yorker* magazine over the pseudonym "Searchlight" between April 4, 1925, and October 2, 1926. Most of the articles written during this period are reprinted in collections which are identified later at their time of publication, as is the one published play.

On August 19, in Notebook IX, Frank wrote a long analysis of his future program, since he felt at thirty-six that he was "once again at a beginning," and in it he stated clearly the premises for the writing of this next period. He began by rejecting the occultist techniques for living, which he had been studying, because his nature elected "the actual forms of human experience" for the expression of the universal. "I aspire to express the Divine *within* the human sphere," he wrote; "I resist the temptations of any golden way or short-cut to cosmic knowledge or cosmic participation, beyond what as a man I may normally exploit. . . . I am not alone a naturalistic mystic—but as well a *realistic* mystic. I propose by my activity to generate cosmic knowledge & divine vision *within* the human domain—not, as in many religious activities employ this impulse to know as an incentive to escape." Occultist techniques, for example, tend to deplete man by displacing the will whereas a true "evolutionary" method may enable man to transcend himself organically "by a complete filling of the content of man" instead of a depleting of it.

The basic assumption in this "evolutionary" method is that "absolute consciousness can be obtained on the phenomenal plane, since all phenomena–unreal of themselves–are functions of the Absolute. Their reality is a result of relation–of a harmony which fuses their intrinsic discords." A theory of esthetics is a natural corollary: "Beauty is, therefore, at once the destiny of all Phenomena and the Value to be discerned in them. . . . As all Phenomena are fused into conscious Beauty, by means of art, they become a unified series of true words by which man, living in phenomenal terms, knows and expresses absolute values."

The fleeting syntheses of history, such as medieval Roman Catholicism, failed because they were based upon exclusions. "The next synthesis must rest upon such general grounds as the fusion of Relativity & the Absolute, of History, psychology, idealism & behaviorism—& on the profound awareness of the relation between the subjective (science, mathematics, etc.) & the objective (the intuition of Absolute reality)."

From this base will rise a new ethic grounded on unity rather than on multiplicity, an art that transfigures phenomena into true values, and "An attitude toward 'Progress & Reform'—individual & social—not in contradiction with the knowledge of Reality as beyond change but illumined & guided by this knowledge." It will be Waldo Frank's function as an artist to create the words which will transfigure the phenomena of the true world of experience, and this task will entail a greater concern than heretofore with social problems.

Having already started on his career as a cultural critic with the *New Yorker* profiles, Frank was named a contributing editor to the *New Republic* in the issue of November 25, 1925, a position he held until 1940. In March, 1926, Jonathan Cape published in London *Virgin Spain*, a remarkable study in cultural history which carried Frank's name throughout America Hispana.

I *Willful Spain*

In his notebooks for *Virgin Spain*, Frank reveals in his early conceptions of the book his plan to make it a drama of the expulsion of the Jews and a lament for the tragic land. His research, however, led him beyond the emotion of his personal identification with Judaism to recognition of the role that the Jews played in Spain; and so the book becomes, as the subtitle indicates, a collection of "Scenes from the Spiritual Drama of a Great People." It is, moreover, a spiritual drama in a musical form. Frank attempts to write what he calls "a Symphonic History" because, as he explains in his acknowledgments, the Personality of Spain holds all of the elements, such as geography, history, laws, art and customs, "*immediately*, as a body holds all its organs." He has, therefore, tried to "let them come, each in its measure and its turn, upon the scene: and like actors in a play, like themes in a symphony, they have spoken their parts."[1] Accordingly, Frank does not describe or analyze these elements of Spain in chronological order. The result is that *Virgin Spain* is not a travel book, but a dramatic tone poem.

The form is ideal for the fullest expression of Frank's best talents as a writer since it permits the use of the lyrical, expressionistic prose of the novels in his depiction of the drama of Spain in terms of his philosophical concept of wholeness. After a brief Prelude, which sings of the Sky of Spain—"Its apartness is a force lifting the broken things of Spain as in a great dance Godward"—and which places the narrator in the scene—"I shall love this people and this world"—Part One pictures, synchronously and expressionistically, regions of modern Spain, each with a personality of its own, sketched against the backdrop of their history.

"Hinterland in Africa" introduces the Moslem theme—Frank believes Modern Spain is more influenced by Africa and the Orient than by Europe—in a poetic word picture of an oasis, a place where the irony of the magic of the desert becomes a smile, just enough of a smile "to tempt man to live on within the toils of the desert." Near the oasis is a town, an Arab world with its market place, swarming with merchants and beggars, half-naked, sore-eyed children, a blind singer, plodding camels, and over all the cry of the muezzin. The reader moves into a house, a cavern after the bright street; there is no furniture, no chimney—"Allah takes care of the smoke." Then he visits the roof, the domain of the women, gay with their colors. From there he watches the women washing clothes in the river: "Other women lay the washed clothes on rocks and with bare feet dance on them, mangling and rinsing in song. . . . Allah is far away, and the pure violence of Mohammed. Women are pagans again. . . . Girls let fall their tunics and their breasts dance with their feet."

With the night comes music: "Drone of men in prayer, sudden motley of boys who sit in a black room and shout the Koran, girl laughter, donkey bray, banter—a music secret as this world." A late worker jogs by on a burro, past the houses of prostitutes: "Now, the classic song of lust. . . . One note for all prayer, one note for all begging, one note for lust. Allah is one." In a large windowless house, belly dancers writhe nude to shrilling pipes. The music falls, and the town sleeps.

The Moslem theme is elaborated with scenes from the Moghreb, where "the archaic world lies whole. . . ." Classic Islam is portrayed as an Idea, an Idea in motion, not essentially as a religion; but the Idea has no place for inner energy since thought and vision are fixed by the Koran, and there is no "method for the creating of ideas whereby life is recreated." Thus, "the Idea of Islam has forbidden its own growth," and "the religion of the Koran is a caricature of God drawn in the lying lines of time and space."

Islam moves into southern Spain, into what is now Andalusia; and the invaders are absorbed "in the mute, indefeasible mass of Spain. . . ." But "the Idea of Islam touched into new intensity the Ideas of Jew and Christian"; and they made war, "a war not of bloods but of souls." These are, however, only the opening scenes of the play; its tragedy begins after the clash of arms ends.

The first and last home of the Moslems in Spain is described by revealing the presence of the past in the cities of Andalusia. In Córdoba, "an eye within the face of Spain," the Idea of Islam lives in the cathedral and in the streets. A woman sings, accompanied by a guitar, to a crowd gathered in the bull-ring; and "this Andalusian song of many wills becomes the drama of Spain." Granada, "the least Spanish of the towns," has the heart of the Moors and "the wreckage of the Moorish body"—Alhambra, which "exiles both the earth and heaven." Seville is an "autoerotic, self-rapt goddess" whose god is Don Juan. But the cities are only parts of the whole; and so the tour of Andalusia closes with dancing, first a gypsy dance, then a classic dance—"this quickened fusion of many hostile worlds into a single Beauty"—and finally, a *flamenco*. Frank's prose style is brilliant in these passages. The dancer's movements are recorded with the detail of a still life and yet the sense of motion of film. Language and form are kept simple and controlled, like the dance; but there is also movement and emotion. The artistry alone justifies these descriptions, but they are also justified by Frank's concept of a nation's history, which finds in the arts a more revealing and significant element of that history than in statistics of production.

The scene now shifts abruptly to "the atom" of Aragon, home of the aboriginal Spaniard—as "unchanged as his mountains." Lacking the elements for the creating of an indigenous culture, Aragon remains prehistoric, only its primal core surviving the "racy cultures" of Italy, Africa, and France which engulfed it. In bright contrast is the variety of Castile: Burgos, whose famous castle dominates the town and casts its shadow over the "city dwelling" of the Cid, "the first hero of Castile," who "reminds us vividly how far his Spain was yet from the ultimate, classic Spanish character, four hundred years after the battle had begun between the Moor and Christian." Salamanca becomes "the city of the Wisdom and the Love of God," whose university blended together East and West: "For the body of Catholic Europe was bone of Greek logic, flesh of Jewish faith and eye of Arab science." The church of Rome was saved when its medieval unity was challenged by the Protestant heresy, and "from Salamanca spread the religious energy which won all South America and part of North America to Roman Doctrine." Here, too, the spirit of the Medieval Synthesis was recreated, the Spirit which still exists in the modern world.

By contrast, Segovia exhibits the complex unity of Spain in the juxtaposition of its cathedral, the Alcázar, and the Roman water bridge; the pragmatic Roman built confidently with no concern for symbol or miracle while the passionate Segovian constructed his chaos with concern for miracle elsewhere. Spain's "unconscious" art weaves the elements of its cross-grained will into a living balance, and "the miracle is born of the unwitting marriage of these wills." Toledo, city of "a Creed and a Rite," symbolizes the mood of the Christian warrior and of El Greco, the mood behind the expulsion of the Jew and the artist's expression of the "Christian Synthesis of Europe at its highest luminous pitch." Two surviving synagogues in the city prompt Frank to write lovingly and eloquently of the Jew in Spain, a "master" for four centuries, who built in the towns "centers of liberal, luxuriant culture" and who kindled a "fire to warm the world and to illumine heaven." The Jew gave a color and a theme to Toledo, and El Greco used them to transfigure the stones of the churches of the city.

But the ultimate word of Castile is entombed in the Escorial, the monument Philip II built to his dream of unity, to "a Spain that was to be the symphony . . . of a hundred peoples and a hundred tongues fused in the grace of Christ," only to discover that "the health of Unity . . must be sought elsewhere." Act One of the drama is nearing its curtain: a glance at Valencia, Spain's dream of a city on the eastern coast, its life now a masquerade, and the curtain falls.

The Second Act, "The Tragedy of Spain," traces the historical background and the genesis of the modern synthesis responsible for the tragedy. The tragic flaw is found in the human will—the paradoxical, misdirected, misused will of the Catholic kings, of saint and sinner, of Don Quixote, and of God. Among the Catholic kings the only significant will proves to be that of a queen—Queen Isabel of Castile, whose "will is Spain." She "works like an artist" to create a unified Spain: "For he alone is the true artist whose personal will is the will of his land and of God" and "only in this marriage of wills can there be true creation." Isabel has the logic and the integrity of the artist but her vision is destructive. She creates "a modern State with a medieval God." Spain is disrupted by the "free life of inimical ideas"; the Inquisition brings "unity in Christ, enforced by the power of the modern state." Her marauding mariners seize "recruits for Christ——and gold for the winning and holding of more recruits": "Isabel's art reaches its ironic climax. Spain's hunger for unity was the hunger for peace. Disunion and multiplicity had made perpetual war. Now unity was achieved, the Spanish rhythm——which was war ——went on. The new ideal nourished the old mode. Spain is the apostle of Christ. Spain has become a state to establish Christ on earth. Let Spain not rest. Christ brings not peace, but a sword." In the vision and the will of Isabel lies the tragedy of Spain.

Spain's "will to union breaks her into extremes," the extremes of will of saint and sinner. "Charity is practiced with the sword and the mystic walks with the thief." The individual Spaniard is a Person in Frank's definition; he knows spiritual unity; but this knowledge only intensifies his drive for social unity—to make others also know, so that he can find his place in the world of men. His need to resist the social chaos of his land is evident in the Spanish sense of honor and in the literature of the age, whether the writings of mystics or the histories of rogues. The mystics of Catholic Spain, who in act and word expressed the will of Isabel, embody Frank's esthetics; in fact, this study of them for the book strongly influences the development of his theory of art: "The process of art is the endowment of a particular experience with the full measure of life. The work of art is a fragment of word or substance informed with the wholeness of spiritual vision. The mystics of Spain were fated to make art, or to make deeds."

The will of Isabel finds militant expression in the Jesuit and in the jurist. The Jesuits "take the Christian mystery as a present truth," and the sword becomes "a mystic instrument." The jurist —Fray Francisco de Vitoria—lays down a rationale of justice; and "that supreme apologia for villainy and greed——International Law——is born and baptized under Christ." The way is clear for Spain to invent the Moral War.

The Spain of Isabel, Carlos, and Philip II is great in idea and Will, which bind the world with God; but the country is squalid in fact: "She was full of heroes and of saints. But the land was arid with neglect. . . . The crass and earthly elements of Spain are not destroyed nor repressed by her religious will: they are engaged . . . . brutality and lust assume in a particular form the wholeness of Spain's will." The sheer impulse of her adventuring is embodied in the *pícaro*, the rogue who personifies the brutality of Spain's methods. Lazarillo de Tormes "is an inverted consciousness of Spain . . .":

> This consciousness is marked by irony: and irony is in the weave of every picaresque design. For the Spanish rascal is no mere reaction from heroic gesture. He is reversion as well. He is moved by the same energy that has uprisen in the forms of asceticism and crusade. His antiphony is but a subtle swerving back from the life he wars on, to Spain's common base. The pícaro has the resource, the intensity, the method, of conquistador and crusader: he preys on his own land. He has the passionateness of the saint: it is directed toward woman. He is a casuist like the Jesuit: his aim is to filch a purse. He navigates uncharted wastes like Columbus: to fill his belly and to save his skin. This continuous awareness of Spain's noble world, this subtle swerve transforming it into villainy and lust, make the ironic pattern. The low

tricks of the pícaro, weaving through the high fabric of his land, once more limn Spain in her fullness.

The greatest heirs of the *pícaro* of Spain appear in Russia—the other extreme of Europe in which energy has become aspirant —in the hero of *Dead Souls* and in the mystic criminals of Dostoevsky.

Velázquez, whose career falls in the reign of Philip IV, "incarnates Spain's desire to be Europe." But as Velázquez molds this desire into an organic form that has the traits of modern Europe, his king loses the Northern and Latin territories: "Europe, accepting the world of appearance as the entire world, pours all its energy to the creating of the immense material universe which is our shambles of the machine and applied science. Spain does not follow."

It is Cervantes, however, who gives the failure of Spain universal implications. "The Will of Don Quixote" becomes "a divine farce, a sort of comic Mystery" within the larger tragic drama of not only Spain but of the modern world. Paraphrase cannot do justice to the matter or manner of these chapters. History, philosophy, psychology, and literary criticism are brilliantly fused in an analysis of medievalism and of literary art which is the climax of the drama. On one level *Don Quixote* depicts the farcical though heroic attempt of Spain "to revive chivalry, to recreate Christ, to re-establish all the world as Christ's Rock and Church. . . ." But on another level the Sorrowful Knight, a medieval "ridiculous Christ," personifies "Frustrate brilliance, seeking to be healed," which "is the one unity of the modern story."

In comparable fashion modern man has sought in vain the salvation of wholeness:

> From our search has come the national concept of the State, for instance: a degenerate medievalism, this——a wistful effort to achieve the wholeness of Rome without the holiness that informed it. Has come the Marxian Internation——an inverted idealism which put up the economic process in place of the Hegelian Spirit. Has come the faith in science as Revelation. Has come, with Rousseau, the seeking of salvation through the return to the unity of man's primordial needs: with Nietzsche, the same seeking in the but seeming opposite direction of the superman. And finally, Darwin inspired us to hope that God might be inserted as the principle of flux in biologic process. All these prophecies and dogmatic actions strove alike to enlist mankind once more in a full unity of life and impulse. All who believed in them, to the extent of their devotion, have been Quixotes.

Men have struggled for five hundred years to construct a unified world with materials as inadequate as the old "magics" of Quixote: "The primacy of reason or of subjective intuition, the autonomy of science or of economic purpose, the ideal of the State or social interstate, the dream of communism or the return to nature. . . ." These "magics" have proved to be as important, unreal, and absurd as the old knight's because they depend upon the personal will to achieve synthesis: "The personal will, in its endeavor to achieve fusion with the world, has concocted formulae that were to act directly on the world, and by magic to control it." Thus Don Quixote, "the last prophet of our historic Order," reveals to Waldo Frank, prophet of our modern order, what we need: "a dynamic understanding which shall enlist ideal and reason, thought and act, knowledge and experience; which shall preserve the personal within the mystical will; which shall unite the world of fact in which we suffer all together, with the world of dream in which we are alone. . . ."

"The Will of God," the last section of Part Two, is an ironic epilogue to the tragedy of Spain personified in Don Quixote. In two synthesizing chapters, "The Bull Fight" and "Man and Woman," Frank portrays in particular events and persons the perversion of the will of God which is responsible for the tragedy. He sees the bull fight as a "gross comedy of blood," in which "Spain's warring elements reach their locked fusion. . . ." Having lived on war for too many ages, the Spanish soul cannot do without conflict. But, "like life in Spain, this spectacle is self-sufficient, issueless. . . ." The *corrida* is an image of static stability, the unique quality of Spanish character known as *personalismo*, which Frank describes in "Man and Woman." Forced to become a person in defense against the chaos of elements in Spain, the Spaniard sees "the world only in terms of himself." He elects a form of achievement and of truth that he can reach—"the simple fusion in every Spaniard of thought and faith, according to a fixed ideal" embodied in the Church of Rome—and then, his energy spent, he goes to sleep. Locked now in his willed equilibrium, the Spaniard lacks the sense of incompleteness of the Frenchman or the Jew, which has a social dimension: "the automatic flow of individual energy into social channels. . . ." Hence the Spaniard, the most willful and intellectual of men, appears will-less and unintelligent. Thus, by default, the "land has become a matriarchy. . . ." The Spanish woman, serene and pragmatic, "erects a great simplicity in which her man can dwell."

In a land incapable of social institutions, she "leans on the Church of Rome," making it Spanish and using it to guide her in molding the family and in materializing the magic words—State, God, Honor—which in the mouth of her man bespeak inaction. Unemotional, unmystical, uncomplicated, she accommodates rather than agitates; and thereby she leaves undisturbed the "dark and dreamless slumber" of Spain.

What will rouse the sleeping giant? Part Three, "Beyond Spain," gropes for an answer. The great cathedral of Barcelona bespeaks a mood of wakefulness, of a beauty that is not tragic. "The Catalan of Spain is an outsider within the gates." Perhaps the same spirit of resistance in the Catalans, which once roused Aragon and Castile to help create Spain, will again disturb the Spanish sleep. Or the peculiar people in the North, the Basques, whose genius for comedy inspired their evasion of the tragic world of their Catholic neighbors, may now invade the life of Spain. Finally, there are the "awakeners" in art and letters—Unamuno, Picasso, Jimenez—who may rouse Spain from her old ordered sleep.

But, even if Spain continues to slumber, she has something of inestimable value for the modern world. In the dialogue between Cervantes and Columbus, which closes the book, Columbus says that "Europe has rotted at last into the Grave they called America" and that Spain must give her spirit to the New World so that it may surpass her. Spain has preserved religious and esthetic values which Frank believes the new world must have to prevent its materialism from digging a grave for the dreams of Europe. Columbus answers the savage despair of Cervantes with a cry of hope: "When they have learned that they can not succeed: that all the Towers and all the machines and all the gold on earth can not crush down this unborn need in them for a true New World——then it will arise." In the second edition of the book (1942), Frank modifies, however, this optimistic prediction because the Spanish Civil War had crushed the impulses toward a new awakening.

Whatever the eventual fate of Spain, the book is a masterpiece of cultural history. In singing prose it reveals the beauty and ugliness of a great and tragic people. Frank loves the land and its folk; loves Spain for its cultivation of things of the spirit; loves the Spaniard for his feeling for life, for his touch with both earth and sky, for his intuitive knowledge of the essentials of wholeness. But Frank's love is not blind; it sees the crippling flaw in the Spanish character and holds it responsible for the tragedy of Spain. He understands the Spaniard but he makes a judgment; he deplores but does not condemn. Spain stands revealed in the height of its achievement and the depth of its failure. The enigma is resolved, and in its place the spirit of Spain flames like a beacon to guide the people of the new world out of their materialistic waste land.

Frank's method is not analytical but esthetic. His creative imagination controls his selection of material; his art gives life, meaning, and form to the elements chosen. Architecture, music, dance, painting, literature, politics, religion, psychology, war, kings, queens, priests, painters, bull fighters and rogues—these reveal the mores, ideas, and values of a culture more clearly and profoundly than surveys or statistics. There is little documentation in *Virgin Spain*; facts are dramatized rather than analyzed; the past is used to explain the present and to suggest the future. Art captures the elusive essence of a chaotic land and a confused people.

Frank's artistic achievement in *Virgin Spain*, however, like Spain's achievement of a static unity, had ironic consequences. His book was disparaged or dismissed in the United States, except by a few critics who knew Spain well; but it was enthusiastically acclaimed in Spain and Latin America. Today editions of Spanish translations keep the book in print, even in Franco Spain, although only the text of the first edition is permitted there. While some readers criticize Frank's philosophy and certain of his social views in *Virgin Spain*, most Spaniards admire the book and accord its author the respect and acclaim denied him in his own country. They feel that he understands the Spanish character and culture better than any other American writer; they continue to buy and read his books, including the novels, although most of them are now out of print in the United States. Frederico de Onís suggests the attitude of most Spaniards in his comment on *Virgin Spain*: "Many of the details may be controversial . . . but the vision in its totality is true and penetrating. Frank's poetic perception conveys to us as no other has done the true reality of Spain, the dramatic reality of a nation which ever consists not in what it is but in what it wills to be."[2]

Virgin Spain not only won an enthusiastic audience for Frank throughout Hispana, but also inspired plans for his study of Latin America, which in turn led to lecture tours in South America and to his subsequent cultural studies of Spanish influence in the southern hemisphere. The result is that Waldo Frank is as widely known in those lands as any American writer. In terms of personal development, as Kloucek notes, *Virgin Spain* intensified Frank's growing awareness "that social consciousness must come before complete self-consciousness, that the individual must act in the world."[3] Frank's discovery of Spain confirms the mystical assumptions in his philosophy but also reveals their relevance to the world of action.

> The Spaniard lacked technic and method to articulate his whole nature in terms of contemporary life; but at least he had not gone off at sterile and dangerous tangents. . . .
>
> He had never succumbed to the superstition that Newton's mechanist laws were the ultimate; and that color and an individual's emotion are on a lower level of reality than mass or gravitation. The West now was also ready—even its physics: Einstein over Newton—to supplant mechanolatry. But only after what injury to the substance of man! what immediate peril!
>
> Frank's idea was not that Spain be imitated or emulated . . It was simply that if the Americans saw the perpendicular vigor of the Spaniard . . . they would sense what was needed and missing in their own way of life. How could the Americas become a New World (rather than the grave of Europe) unless they produced new men?[4]

Our America exhibits Frank's potential as a cultural critic; *Virgin Spain* fulfills that potential.

CHAPTER 5

The Searchlight on Culture

THE CREATIVE DRIVE toward cultural studies which produced nearly a hundred articles during the writing of *Virgin Spain* continued after the publication of the book. In May, 1926, Frank became contributing editor to *New Masses*, beginning with its first issue; and he held the position until February, 1930. During May, he took a brief vacation, visiting Cuba and the Isle of Pines with Hart Crane. Upon his return to New York, he experienced a characteristic sense of emptiness and depression and jotted in his notebook a reason for his mood: "Isolatedly superior to the mob of readers & of writers, I am passionately one with them all in their disdain for me." Still haunted by his desire to be a novelist, he tried to work on the narrative that he had promised Liveright, but it was to be 1934 before he finished *The Death and Birth of David Markand*. In September, he wrote in two weeks *Flamingo Isle*, a five-act comedy; but it remains unpublished. In November, *Time Exposures by Search-Light*, a collection of his *New Yorker* sketches, was published anonymously.

I *Profiles*

The facetious subtitle for the volume summarizes the contents and suggests the tone: "*Being Portraits* of Twenty Men and Women *famous* in Our Day *together with* Caricatures *of the* Same *by* Divers Artists *to which is appended* An Account of a Joint Report *Made to* Jehovah *on the* Condition *of* Man *in the* City *of* New York [1926] by Julius Caesar, Aristotle *and a* Third Individual *of* Less Importance."[1] Some of the better known of those twenty men and women are Otto Kahn, William Lyon Phelps, Georgia O'Keeffe, Ignace Paderewski, Carl Sandburg, Charles Chaplin, John Dewey, Sinclair Lewis, Theodore Dreiser, Katharine Cornell, and Alfred Stieglitz.

The mildly satiric tone of these profiles is established in the

Foreword in which Search-Light asks forgiveness of his former friends if "these impertinent portrayals" offend them. The editors of *The New Yorker*—"these ribald, irreverent, practical" gentlemen—are responsible. They have bribed poor Search-Light to shine upon his friends; and, since he has never before "written *anything* for money," he is not to blame for "the infamies herein recorded."

In keeping with the tone, Frank employs a style in these portraits that is relaxed, descriptive, and witty, without the intensity or lyricism of the novels or histories. But the bland style does not blunt his perceptions, and the character sketches of individuals create a satirical portrait of contemporary culture: "Through the Wall Street canyon, Kahn blows like a zephyr. Under the looming granite walls, he walks with round cheeks. Our world is a delirium of electric blares: Kahn's eyes twinkle. Our world is a holocaust of dying civilizations: Kahn knows not of death. He is a happy lover, lyrical and unattached."

Sinclair Lewis is the image of America: "hungry, restless, yearning in some unuttered way to do, to create, to serve." He also satisfies in his fiction the desires stirred by a strange duality about America:

> She is passionately in love with herself, and is ashamed of herself. Mystically sure that she is the greatest thing on earth, she gives her open admiration only to what is far away or what is patently mediocre. She is arrogant——and obsequious; cocksure——and faltering; boastful——and dumb. Above all, she is adventurous——and afraid. . . .
>
> Now, deep in her heart America had a secret. It was this: Loving herself, loving . . . every vulgar ludicrous detail of her unstoried life, she was ashamed to admit this. . . . And what she wanted was a way whereby she could love herself, and yet *seem* to be doing just the opposite. . . . Some subtle sense of better things barred her from flagrant flaunting of her self-adoration; but in no way destroyed her hidden passion to caress her own junk-pile towns, her junk-pile business men, her blatant morals and her strident arts. . . .
>
> Sinclair Lewis, heaven-sent, solved the mighty problem; gave to his Mother herself in a form which she could relish unblushingly at last! . . . America wanted her Main Street. And the rage in which it came clad by Sinclair Lewis saved her Puritan shame. Taking the anger along, she could revel at last in this body of herself. . . .
>
> For this is the secret of his success. To America, Puritan, moralizing, fiercely auto-erotic, he gave herself to worship in a

guise she could accept. The love of self-identification informs his portraits of American dullness. And the lyricism of external denunciation makes them acceptable to American dullards who, shamefacedly aware of themselves, are yet in love with themselves. And makes them acceptable to all the world! . . .

Sometimes social criticism is expressed in terms of Frank's philosophy of the Person, as in his portrait of "An Entire Person":

> Description and analysis won't get us Katharine Cornell. . . . A part of her is not a key to her. *Wholeness* is in each of her aspects.
>
> Perhaps this explains, somewhat, her place in the synthetic world of Broadway. Parts are so common in this life of ours which is indeed a stage. Wholes are so rare. The world's run largely by *partial* people: folk who can do just this, just that; . . . little bits of men and women who assemble the Machine Age as if they were individual nuts, cranks, gears and levers. Yet despite the Machine and the fate of us all to do our part in it ——our so replaceable part——we are still hungry for another kind of world: for the world of spirit in which each one of us is not a part, not replaceable; but in some mystic way is entire and is eternal.

In the "Joint Report," which ends the book, Caesar and Aristotle praise the mechanical marvels of earth. Aristotle is especially impressed by the order and uniformity of the New Yorker's intellectual life: "At first I believed that there must be one prolific and ubiquitous dictator who wrote all their books under a thousand names, preached simultaneously in church and synagogue, directed the platforms of opposition parties, taught . . . in all the universities. . . . They are uniform, indeed. They tolerate no idea which runs radically counter to their complacent rhythm. . . . They have one Value, one Ideal: and no word rises against them." But God's pleasure in the report is disturbed by the words of a newcomer, Spinoza, who claims that he found in the earth people only confusion, turmoil, chaos: "A pitiful knocking about, and longing . . . . and the sum of it all was bitter emptiness." Thus, *Time Exposures* reveals, despite its different tone and style, the characteristic tenets of Frank's philosophy and social criticism.

II *A Play*

Still determined to write the novel about Markand, Frank went to Europe in January, 1927, to travel, meditate, and wait for the book to emerge from his unconscious. While he was visiting

Heidelberg and Berlin, he wrote a series of articles for *McCall's*, revised *Flamingo Isle*, and worked on the novel. In March, Frank married Alma Magoon in Paris, a little over a year after his divorce from Margaret Naumburg; they traveled through southern France to Egypt and Palestine. They returned to France in June and settled at St. Georges d'Oléron, where Frank, resisting the temptation to write about Judaism, plunged into the novel and completed a fifty-thousand word draft. By September the Franks were back in New York, and Frank put the novel aside to work on the articles for the *New Republic* which grew into his next book, *The Re-discovery of America*. He also gave a series of lectures on modern art at the New School for Social Research.

Throughout 1928, he worked hard on *The Re-discovery of America*, the chapters appearing regularly in the *New Republic* as part of a kind of "Our America—Second Series," which Herbert Croly had suggested. Frank refused to do a similar series for the *Saturday Evening Post* even at its generous rates. In November, *New Year's Eve*, the play Frank had been writing since 1919, appeared in *Second American Caravan*, published November 29, 1928.

The play gets its title from the time of the action—New Year's Eve of the twentieth century; but two rejected titles for it—"Birth" and "The Healing"—derive from the theme previously articulated in the lyric novels: life is a wound, a bleeding, which can be healed only by full participation in it. This theme is developed in seven scenes which portray the tragic consequences of a nobly-intentioned lie, involving the paternity of an unborn child. As the play opens, the lovers deny the paternity; and the resulting unhappy marriages poison the lives of several family groups. A double suicide forces the confession and the climax when the assumed father must decide to accept the love which life brings along with its woes. Revelation forces an ultimate acceptance that is both the real fruit of living and of life's healing.

Unfortunately, the theme does not prove as viable in play form as in the lyric novels. Nor does Frank's generally dramatic style lend itself to effective prose for the stage. The dialogue in *New Year's Eve* is mannered and forced; the characters are wooden and one-dimensional. The use of a chorus to chant refrains such as "Life is holy" and "This is the healing of life" simply contributes to the artificiality of the whole. Nevertheless, the Group Theater, in its self-conscious search for serious dramas, gave the play a private, try-out performance before dropping it from the production schedule. Scribner's, however, published the text in 1929, the only one of Frank's ten plays to be printed.

III *Return to Our America*

In March, 1929, Scribner's also published *The Re-discovery of America; an Introduction to a Philosophy of American Life.* It is "a book without charm," Frank warns in his preface, "a book almost fleshless and with no smiles or pleasant moods at all. . . . The Europe I love is not pictured in it; nor the feature, trait and voice of the America I love."[2] As the subtitle suggests, this study has a philosophical objective whereas *Our America* and *Virgin Spain* are critical interpretations of cultures; consequently, *Re-discovery* is more didactic and abstract than the cultural histories, and its style is less colorful. It goes beyond the histories, however, in its exploration in Part Three of the potentialities for a new synthesis of creative forces which will resolve the chaos of American life.

Part One, "Causes and Conditions," sketches the dissolution of modern Europe as it discarded the general convictions—previously outlined in the essay "For a Declaration of War"—which underlay the unity of the medieval age and constituted then "the spiritual anatomy of Europe," the laws by which men "created beauty and found truth." The disintegration of religion and the triumph of science symbolize the loss of a sense of the Whole, the prelude to cultural decay and death: "Religion and politics must form a whole, if either is to be a part of health." The medieval synthesis was "the first conscious attempt of occidental man to create with all the man and with all men an embodied spiritual Whole."

Modern science, "a structure based on the revelation of the senses," shatters the wholeness, which had been contingent upon God alone; and it pieces together a multiverse turned horizontal instead of vertical, toppling the Gothic spires. "Progress within human limits was invented to displace the old religious progress that had led direct from man to angel. . . . Action within this new infinity became the norm and the end." The machine replaces God, and the personal will, dissociated from a spiritual whole, worships the machine, the "most perfect symbol of personal desire. . . ." But "The spread of the machine in a world where the machine expresses personal wills that are not *themselves* integrated by the sense of the Whole, can only be the 'progress' of chaos."

Thus, the United States, dedicated to this limited concept of "progress," becomes the "grave of Europe," the final resting place of the Old World's fragmented parts. Social, political, and religious customs, already decaying in the Old World, are transplanted to the new and kept alive in isolated plots: New England, the South, the Bible Belt:

> America became a land of men possessed of little remnants of an ideal Whole. . . . Each of these fragments, assuming the entire energy of Truth, grew domineering. The individualism and *laissez-faire* of England became an atomism. The equalitarianism of France . . . became the herd chaos of Jacksonian democracy. The sects of the dissolving European Church became the ambulant madhouses that dotted the farm-land from Oneida to Salt Lake. The rationalism of European science, whose founders had openly declared allegiance to some mystic faith, shrank with us into an atheistical religion that stuck the universe within the pigeon-hole of its own logic. Finally, the bourgeois movements of industrialised Europe became the frantic property-ism of the American towns.

The rotting of the transplanted parts of Europe releases the individual for action which creates little more than motion. Man is truly alone, since he is now without any contact with an organic whole: "The American of the emerging twentieth century was the loneliest man in the world: the world of his fathers had vanished, and no America had been created to replace it."

Part Two—"Facts"—is a probing analysis of contemporary life in which the author dissects the American mind and social institutions. Using a favorite image, the jungle, to symbolize the cultural condition, Frank likens the American to the savage whose "conceptual knowledge of the world about him is but the exteriorisation of his personal sense." The rankest growth in this jungle is the machine: "Nature for the American is this iron chaos of life-providing, death-dealing, value-distilling forces." The machine alone among the legacies of Europe thrives, because it "alone is a positive expression of the personal will freed from the dissolving synthesis of Europe." The other cultural deposits—"our religions, our arts, our ideals of equality and freedom—were all *fragmented* expressions, not of the personal will, but of that Whole. As that Whole dissolved, they dissolved." Their dissolution more fully releases the personal atom for personal aggrandizement through the machine, which embodies personal will and willful action. "We know that from the machine's need to expand has grown our ideology of persuasion, our hideous myth of 'progress' as an external matter: that man's life is becoming more and more the pitiful rationale of the machine." The fragmentary "self," motivated now only by personal desire, sets up a world of its own in which it performs like a machine: "Our jungle is a nature of machines. *We are the hunted in our jungle, because this world of ours is the exteriorisation of our own desire. Our nature is aggressive, because it is the embodied action of our aggressive will. We are subject to this jungle, we adore it and we feed it with our lives, because it is quite literally ourselves.*"

For the individual who accepts only himself, the will-to-power is God: "Power is the imposition of the one upon the external world. . . . All outside this one must submit or be destroyed. Power is the expression of the brute, of the savage, of the child —of any being whose self-awareness has not spread beyond the majesty of personal will." Therefore, a mass of power-persons cannot integrate to form a true society; they can form only a herd of self-assertive atoms. For they lack the creative power of Love —sexual, intellectual, social, esthetic, mystic—which alone makes possible the fusion that transcends the self. Thus America dissipates its potential for becoming a true society, a Whole, by striving for Unity through the exercise of Power instead of Love:

> It legislates, it organizes, it marshals loyalty into institutions which, serving specific ends, are mere machines. It endeavours, that is, to *force* our birth and our growth. Thus, we enact laws regulating morals; thus gather in Rotary Clubs and Ku Klux Klans. Our purpose is good, it is to create a spiritual active Whole from the chaos which we feel within us. But since the means we use is Power—child of chaos—we perpetuate our chaos. Power can render homogeneous, for its way is to destroy or cause to submit what differs from it. But uniformity is the contrary of integration. Stirring to be born, we apply Power and bring death; restless in our herd-state, we force Power on the herd and confirm it. . . .

The worship of Power renders man paradoxically servile and passive. Having accepted the sovereignty of Power, the individual is predisposed to accept a greater Power than his own in another person or in the mass: the American who is comfortable only in the mob, who distrusts any impulse in himself which cannot be coined in power, who despises minorities. "The reign of Power means a mass of men who have lost freedom and creativity. For the free man is he who has come through the personal (infantile) experience of Power, and the personal need for Power, thereby winning the strength of knowledge that he is part in a Whole: and the creative man is he who understands that the personal will must become a factor in a union that transcends it." But the man of Power is not self-contained, not self-evolving; and he confuses superficial "change" with growth: "The whole man is disengaged, save as the lust of Power can employ him: all that is contemplative, creative, religious in him becomes inert."

In the remaining chapters of Part II, Frank examines the various states of consciousness in which the American tries to "render bearable his intolerable world, not by transfiguring it, but by perfecting an anaesthetic system of substitutes to hide it." In "Gods and Cults of Power," Frank isolates the Power-fact in the pretentious substitutes represented by cults of success: the machine, the efficiency drive, the corporation, fraternal organization, popular literature, art, sports, politics, crime, sex, legislation, official charity, puritanism, spiritualism, theosophy, and psychoanalysis. These pretenses are misplaced desires. Americans give them their energy and their spirit in the hope that they will be fulfilled by them. But they cannot fulfill, since they do not afford opportunities for creative living, being only make-believes of "truth" and "beauty."

Other manifestations of the atomic individual's will to power are examined in chapters on the search for comfort as a value in itself; news as a folk art; current art forms as "in part reflection and apology for our chaos, and in part rebellion from it"; censorship in all of its manifold expressions as a corollary of the Power drive; and, finally, so-called leaders as victims of our chaos. All these stages of consciousness, whatever their form, portray the impact of America's materialistic concept of progress, which ensnares the individual in a struggle for power as the means of fulfillment.

But the power stage, although necessary in the growth of the savage or child, should be only a phase in the development of a new synthesis. Part III of *Re-discovery of America* discusses resources for achieving the higher stages of consciousness in which love supplants power, a feeling of oneness replaces the separatistic ego, and chaos gives way to a social order affording opportunities for fulfillment. In chapters on American women, the

American folk, and the American mystic tradition, Frank discovers potential and promise for the future. He sees women as reverting to *femaleness*, having learned "that no pursuit of man on *his* terms, no cult of Power, brings the indeputable nourishment of love." Man will have to change to win her, will have to learn that love is "the principle of union, of order, of creation"; and this may be the "first step in the creation of a Whole from our American chaos. . . ."

The folk of America, now that its infant stage of preoccupation with belly and hands is passed, "hungers to be a people"; "but Production—newsprint, radio, communication—clamps uniformity upon it. The value . . . becomes the achievement of an inner sameness like the outer sameness of machine-politics, machine-art, machine-sport, machine-customs." Having no conscious standards beyond momentum, the folk confuses movement with programs, rationalizes its aspirations in its leaders, justifies its inertia in the pleasure of conformity, and threatens, through "colossal levelling from downward" to transform "the magnificent dreams of our world into business and bigness." But the "hunger" of the folk to become a varied, integral people is a value in itself which needs only America's great mystic tradition and a method to create a new consciousness.

From its founding, America has had the mystic tradition: a "consciousness of the whole of man and of God . . . which identified the self of our land with the destiny of human kind." Columbus, seeking to make the two halves of the world one, "grounded our mystic tradition." The Puritans "made the tradition organic, by establishing it as the Law. . . ." But the rise of "the 'practical men' who rejected the Whole since it had failed" drove the tradition underground and built the America of Power. However, the tradition did not die; it continued to speak in Lincoln, Emerson, Poe, Thoreau, and Whitman. Since the practical tradition, which nurtures "separateness" in its love of Power, can perpetuate only more chaos, the folk must re-create the mystical tradition in order to establish "the symphonic nation in whom all selves and all visions adumbrate to Wholeness." But the folk needs leaders and a technique if the re-creation of a tradition and a value to *living* is possible. The rest of the book is concerned with the description of a method which will lead to "the creating of a People."

"The method of American life must be the group," Frank declares in the opening paragraph of the chapter entitled "Beginning." And "the method of the group is the person. There can be no integration of America without the group whose sense of the Whole will make it whole: there can be no group without the person whose sense of the Whole is his life." In "Notes on Method," a long subsection of the chapter, Frank discusses how one establishes in himself this sense, which will in turn make group action constructive. By analogy with the archaic methods of Hindu and Jew, one begins by observing himself "as *within the Whole*" by taking his "*body* as within the context of life." It follows that his thoughts and emotions, being of the body, are also within the Whole. Thus, "the person, moved by the image of himself as a focus within the Whole, will act in unison with his sense of the Whole. . . . This man will be beyond the dualisms and dichotomies that have made history a mischief. . . ."

Free of the need for personal aggrandizement and sustained by his sense of cosmos within himself, the Person will grow aware of others like himself in the American chaos and "will commune and converge" with them to create a group, which in turn will beget groups like it. How the group members come together is unimportant: "Perhaps they are all of a single race or of a city block or of a shop; perhaps they have converged to form some revolutionary 'cell'; perhaps they have joined to discover beauty or to worship God. . . . The deliberate change of attitude is what counts: it works its magic upon them." Then for this group America "will be the imagined Whole—the image of a creative nation which it can work out . . . in its own group life," and that group life will join with other group lives, like the single notes in a symphony which "lift their instant voices, and pass," to create the Symphonic Nation.

Since "the actionable Whole is within," the work of the group will for a long time be concerned with experiencing "in the image of its ideal, its own life and thought as a phase of the American nation." Consequently, the group may require a generation in which to prepare itself for political activity. But "as the group becomes more knowing (in its sense of knowledge as organic action) its immediate deed will spread to include behaviour" in public issues.

Frank selects three issues then challenging the American mind and temper to demonstrate the potential nature of group action: the problems posed by Soviet Russia, Latin America, and Europe "should be admirable means for self-search and for union among men." They are also indicative of the future course of

Frank's social thought and action. Russia, for example, is conducting a crucial experiment—"the attempt to raise the base of human life above the nutritive"—and the sole duty of the group should be "to keep hands off and to help with reverent respect." But, if America should elect to threaten "the peace of the high experiment in Russia, it would be the group's business to fight for it——to fight for the truth no matter how close to home were the lie."

Latin America, however, needs a clasped-hands rather than a hands-off policy; for her people have "the persistent strain of the mystic tradition" and the desire to create "an American world that shall be more than the grave of Europe." The group might work for a new doctrine of American union by rejecting the escape mechanism of "regarding these American nations as mere *political* units," by "the undermining of that historic symbol of our impertinence——the Monroe Doctrine," and by promoting "relations of life and art, not of mere political and mercantile technic." The objective is a brotherhood of men, not just a brotherhood of nations; and, "if we choose Love and not Power, life and not death . . . America Latina will join us."

The problem for hostile, receding Europe is the threat of "Americanisation," involving "the traits of the American Jungle and of its cults of Power"—the by-products of the decay of Europe returning to their source. To combat this menace, Europe is searching for a new whole—"*conscious Europeanism*"—which may increase her hostility or make her creative and receptive. Since Americanization is a fact and not a morbid aspiration, Americans alone can overcome it. The compact and actionable group must transfigure the fact if Europe is to rejoin America. If the mechanical and psychological Jungle continues to engulf, "America as a high world is doomed": "For Americanisation is a disease which must disappear, either by our mastery of it or by its mastery of us. If it spreads, the white man will go down. Possibly the sun will rise on a Chinese world, from which this scourge has scourged itself away."

But the most significant point in *The Re-discovery of America* is that America can be saved. The closing passages of the book express both this thought and the optimism of Frank:

> I write these words for those who will look on the possible American doom with a light heart: and not swerve from their task of self-creation and of leadership . . . . they will not let their hands cease from the labour of beauty. . . . Having found wholeness in

themselves, . . . They will act each hour to make themselves more true and to bring truth to bear upon the unborn world: not for any issue in time or person, but for the joy of the eternity of the moment lived in the image of God.

The life of such men will be the fulfillment of America's oldest tradition. And it may be that in their fulfillment a world called America will be discovered.

In a way *Re-discovery of America* is both a summation and a projection. In it Frank finally makes clear the meaning of Wholeness, of the Person, of the mystic, and of the mystical tradition —concepts heretofore shadowy and half-expressed in his writings —and he constructs a method for the future. This formulating of possibilities for action most sharply distinguishes the book from *Our America* and *Virgin Spain*, but there are other differences. It is as critical as *Our America* of the American Jungle, but is also less shrill and more tolerant. A wiser Frank now accepts the Power phase as a condition of growth. The book does lack the charm of *Virgin Spain*, since it has less drama and less portraiture; but its analysis of the American mind is full of insights, and Frank's conception of an organic society is a serious challenge to those who have a vision of what America might become if she finds a new synthesis, one embracing esthetic and spiritual values while permitting the whole man to fulfill himself. The book is indeed "An Introduction to a Philosophy of American Life," and even those who must reject Frank's mystical concepts can find much to admire in it. More critical than esthetic, it brings Frank closer to social action as it crystallizes his ideas about Russia and Latin America, the subjects of his next two books.

IV *South America Discovered*

For a brief time after the publication of *Re-discovery*, Frank suffered the exhaustion, discouragement, and illness which often followed one of his major creative efforts. But, when invitations arrived in April to lecture in Latin America, he left in June for Mexico to start a tour that lasted through December; that took him to Argentina, Bolivia, Peru, Chile, Colombia, Brazil, Uruguay, and Cuba; and that resulted in two more publications: *Primer mensaje a la América Hispana* (the texts of the forty-two lectures given on the tour published in Madrid early in 1930) and *America Hispana: A Portrait and a Prospect* (published by Scribner's in September, 1931).

America Hispana is, like *Re-discovery of America*, an analysis of the effects of transplanting European values onto the soil of the New World, the difference being that it is concerned with the influence in Latin America of the esthetic and religious values of medieval Spain rather than with those of modern Europe. It is also closer to *Virgin Spain* than to *Re-discovery* in style: it is a book with charm and an esthetic function. Frank spells out the latter in his Acknowledgments and, in so doing, reveals something of his theory of form in writing history:

> Like its predecessors in that division of my writings which I call History, this book must be taken as a work of art. The subject is a people, rather than——as in that division which I call Story——a person or group of persons. But the aim is not primarily to give facts or information: it is to create for the reader an image of the living organism about which the facts are recorded, to give him an experience of the truth which this collective living being represents. This is the aesthetic function. Therefore in these books which . . . I may group together as "The New World" ("Our America," "Virgin Spain," "The Rediscovery of America," "America Hispana," etc.), the substance and even the form do not essentially differ from the substance and form of such works as "Rahab" and "City Block." Only the focus differs, being macrocosmic instead of microcosmic as in fiction. Hence, "America Hispana" should be read as one would read a story——or rather, as one would listen to a symphony: sequentially from the beginning to the end.[3]

Since Latin America is such a vast, inchoate mass without the sterile unity of Spain or the seeming homogeneity of the United States, Frank tells its story in terms of peoples and regions which typify some aspect of the whole, and he seeks unity by turning to myth: "In no other work does Frank so fully exploit the telluric forces symbolized by the primordial Earth Mother . . . . the myth governs the structure of the book."[4] Thus, in the Prelude, Frank suggests a mythic unity in Panama, "the relic juncture of two legendary worlds"—Atlantis and Lemuria—and in the Canal a symbol of the potential unity "of two other worlds—the two Americas. . . ." Simon Bolivar dreams of establishing a dual American union, the Atlantic World; but Theodore Roosevelt, the personification of energy in "that infantile form of Power" which mesmerizes the United States, shatters the dream. This historical fact becomes the despair or the hope of the story. Latin America has the spiritual vision; North America has the energy and the technical knowledge; together they can create a new Atlantic World, or, if the United States predominates, another American jungle. The alternatives give the book its dramatic tension.

In keeping with this mythic approach, Frank begins his portrait with the "Children of the Rock," the Indians of the mountains of High Peru, worshippers of stone and sun; and with the "Children of the Sun," the Incas, who "produced what is perhaps the first rational society of man." Having no concept of himself as a separate entity, the Indian found his identity only in his group, his *ayllu*, a communal body rooted in soil and nourished by blood which constituted the atom of selfhood: "All forces, inward and outward, not instrumental to the ayllu as the agent of welfare, were excluded." But, caught in a cycle of communal imagination and communal law, the folk of Peruvian America could not create New Worlds: "It was a lovely pragmatism since the folk was sweet with closeness to the earth and adroit to bloom like flowers in their arid mountains. Yet like all pragmatisms it was doomed. For pragmatism, everywhere, discourages the ideal, and the energy, of transcending the forms which the existent culture chooses as instrumental to its perseverance. In Peru, this took the shape of forbidding the imagination to transcend the group, either within the soul or beyond the Sun."

The will of the group proves to be no match for the personal will of the Spaniard. The conquistador believed in his own person and the divine justification of his own will: "The personal will of a thousand Spaniards pours the energy of all the Mediterranean upon America: energy no longer locked in the Synthesis of Medieval Europe and now released into the unitary channel of those men's personal will." The Indian is overwhelmed; and he settles into the soil, like the Andean rock, to exist by not wanting anything: "To desire things, he has learned, is to be entrapped in the world of the stranger. . . ."

The union of Spaniard and Indian produces the mestizo, who, in Frank's method of writing cultural history, represents one phase of the total problem of Latin America. "The Century of the Mestizo" is a perceptive analysis of this curious byproduct of two "world-wills" who, in searching wildly for a third, creates much of the anarchy of South America:

> The hour of the mestizo is the century of turmoil which has succeeded the Emancipation. . . . The mestizo is expressing himself. In his bewilderment, he is a child: not ready to think or act in terms of law. When he is forced, like a child, he imitates. He

> sets up inappropriate republics; irrelevant constitutions. What he is really doing is to articulate his instinctive needs. . . . For he is a man in whom two worlds are riven in mortal deadlock; and both must die before his own can be born. . . .
>
> When he has created his world, the mestizo . . . will have disappeared . . . . there will be new Americans, instead.

Twinned with this biological heritage is an economic one which has its disruptive effects. In the nineteenth century, foreign capital becomes the ruling power; the new republics crush the native communes and alienate the masses. The demagogues rise to use "the energy of popular despair to swing them into office." But perhaps this exploitation of the masses will make them receptive, also, to the true leader when he comes. Frank feels that the young students give a small hope for future leadership: "The image of an organic world is in them; of an organic *human* world made divine not through denial but through integration, and fulfilled by the experience of the cosmos inherent in each soul."

For another phase of this culture, Frank swings south from Peru, "the heart of colonial South America," to the pampa, whose motion impresses the psyche with the integral co-existence of things instead of their separate reality and fuses a continent with the Atlantic. Frank finds the story of the pampa in the Argentine cities and in the famous gaucho. The latter is especially stimulating to Frank's creative imagination, and he writes eloquently of this semi-mythic figure: "a man in whom the Spanish qualities were redirected." Frank's description of the gaucho dance is a good example of his prose style and his use of the arts in describing cultures:

> The gaucho transformation of the Spanish dance makes this metabolism of the spirit clear. The classic Andalusian dance is solitary (the unit is the person and normally the woman): it is vertical, static, and its beauty has ethical and mystic implications. The dancer expresses the quietude to which her religious will composes the tumultuous world. And this quiet, sculpted of the muscular motions of a woman's body, is the matrix of the dance's beauty and of the dancer's salvation. The gaucho dance is neither solitary like Spain's nor of the group like the Indian dance figures. Two bodies are in continuous flow. The man's feet prance like a horse in gallop on the pampa, but the movement is locally confined, he scarcely moves; the woman's torso stirs like the breast of the pampa in a heavy wind, but she moves not at all. The sum of the subtle weaves of mobility is stillness: the woman is the focus and the man tends toward her.

> This contradiction of the solitary ranger whose dance is a social unit, of the ready fighter whose dance is reticent and chaste, of the despiser of woman whose dance gives to the woman the central place, reveals the gaucho spirit. He is cruel yet tender, he is beyond the law yet a man of law, he is illiterate yet fertile in tradition. And these dichotomies resolve into a fluid, intricate, emotionally concordant person.
>
> . . . . For he is the fluid pampa, and the rock of Castile.

The historic gaucho is dead, a victim of the machine, but not before he has been made immortal in "the greatest folk poem of the modern western world"—*Martin Fierro*. "The gaucho had died in order that the land might have body: he is reborn in order that the body may have spirit."

The Argentine cities reveal the manner in which the European heritage is being transformed, grossly in some, subtly in others. "Here is Tucumán . . . with noises never heard by Spain and the gutters are a tussle of commercial wills, North American in form, Levantine in spirit." In Santiago del Estero, in contrast, "Spain suddenly re-lives . . . . whose will to integrate her peoples here comes magically true." The men of Rafaela, "for all their Latin tongue and their Catholic God . . . are close to the farmers of Iowa and Kansas"; yet "these clodhoppers of the pampa hint at something unborn in them yet old." Buenos Aires, like New York and unlike most capitals of America Hispana, is not a Christian city. Catholic social forms survive, but the Catholic form itself as dogma is dead. "The symbol and god of this world is the machine, its rationale is capitalism. And these war with the old cults in Buenos Aires." There is no such war in Rosario, however, "where the elements of this Atlantic world are more alone . . . . and the lawyers, brokers, politicians . . . look down with pride . . . rejoicing that Rosario is almost as hideous as a city in Ohio."

From the Atlantic community, Frank shifts to the Pacific, whose only symbol is Chile; but the symbol is irrelevant, since Chile, despite its refusal to "look east in spirit," is tightly linked to the Atlantic combine by its dependence upon North American money for its mines. Frank selects Chile to illustrate the evil effects of exploitation by business interests of the United States in Latin America, and he turns to narrative technique for the tale of a young writer's homecoming to dramatize the horrible squalor and degeneracy of the copper miners in an American "company town."

After a brief return to Peru, to describe Lima—"the archetypical mestizo city"—and to characterize the modern dictators and Marxist revolutionaries, Frank follows the Amazon back to the Atlantic and to the promise of Brazil. In Brazil, which "has black Africa within it," will rise, if anywhere, "a new world tropic culture." But this new culture will not come until it breaks the hold of the coffee man whose "idea of Progress for Brazil implies the negation of its folk and its ethos. . . . By Progress he means . . . forcing on Brazil, irrespective of whether they apply, the values and forms of life which have made the United States, industrial Britain and modern Germany, such happy places." Meanwhile, the Negro in the great forests typifies the technical problems of adjustment in Latin America.

The Atlantic now carries Frank through space and time to the Caribbean—"The Central Sea"—and to the Maya, "a culture that soared like a flame to the stars." In a long account of Maya, Aztec, and Mexican cultures, he finds in their myths evidence of the role of earth as primordial mother, a value in their way of life which the United States ignores. "All human culture, like a tree, is rooted in earth, rises in earth; is a transfigured form of the earth substance fertilized by light that is more than earthly. . . ." From earth comes man's bread; from conflict with earth comes man's knowledge of power; from communion with earth comes man's recognition of himself and his place in the Whole. "Bread-power-religion are the triune whole of culture. . . . Without them all in due proportion, a race of men is less than wholly human." Thus the industrial culture of the United States is a fractional one of only bread-and-power in which the individual has lost contact with the soil and the self. The culture of Mexico from Aztec times has neglected bread-and-power while letting religion become hypertrophic. So "across the frontier of Rio Grande, two cultures face each other. Both are incomplete, wanting some crucial element of wholeness; both, in varying degrees, long for completion."

The book closes with an analysis of the "Prospect" for this completion, for the creation of "The Atlantic World" out of the American half-worlds, each needing what the other has. "The problem in the North is one of religion——where the South folk are strong: the problem of the South is one of discipline, technique and method, where the North is strong." The problems can be solved and the new world created, however, only by a transformation in the concept of the Person which will assure the triumph of the spirit. As Frank had shown in *Re-discovery of*

America, the United States lacks true persons; and its machine culture, whose only religion is pragmatism, separates the North American from his soul and soil. Thus he falls short of being the total person because his ideals are not expressed in public action, and "the true person acts as a social being." Consequently, Latin America, like Spain, flounders in chaos; its spiritual seeds are dormant, its morals are shattered.

Yet if these half-worlds are not joined, they will be destroyed by the chaos they create. Frank considers various possibilities for federation, culminating in Austral America, "an Atlantic body in counterpoise to the United States"; but he admits that the prospects are dim and for the ages. Therefore, he turns to the kind of action which can have immediate consequences: "an action that partakes at once of the regeneration of the person and of the ideal for the nation." As in *Re-discovery*, this action involves the production of persons and groups who will live "*personally* the life they would create for America Hispana. . . ." Human re-creation must precede political regeneration, for the practical problem is organic; it is life itself. "For the high promise of America Hispana, in essence, is not the promise of vastly potential races, not the promise of profound traditions, not the need of the Atlantic peoples for just such spiritual redemption as America Hispana seems by its genius capable of bringing: it is the simple challenge to men and to young nations to make of their lives an incarnate quest of the Truth."

The simple challenge stirred Latin Americans, but the challenger won their hearts. Here was an American who criticized severely but did not preach; an American who loved the Spanish world almost as much as his own—for its best qualities while fully aware of its worst ones; an American who came as a brother, speaking the language, understanding the family customs, and asking for help on an exchange basis. Perhaps, as Arnold Chapman suggests, Frank's minority status in his own country, as a Jew and as an intellectual, makes it easier for large numbers of Spanish Americans to accept him "in the role of fellow sufferer and combatant."[5] Whatever the reason, Frank finds "south of the border" his largest and most enthusiastic audience—a phenomenon that in its perpetuation heightens the *irony* of his own country's indifference toward him without making that fact more palatable.[6]

CHAPTER 6

The Social Dimension

DURING THIS PERIOD of his career, Frank's concern for the social projection of man led him away from the lyric novels to cultural criticism; the concern took him back to the novel and at the same time involved him with the Communist conspiracy and a travel book about Russia.

When *America Hispana* went to press, Frank set out in August on a vacation trip which would take him by way of Stockholm to Leningrad, Moscow, Novgorod, then home through Berlin and Paris. Upon his return to New York, he extended his vacation in a way most congenial to him and without the stress of travel: he wrote another book, or rather he let a book write itself: "I resolved not to work on this one: not to organize its materials, not to essentialize its form," he wrote in the opening section.[1] The result, *Dawn In Russia* (1932), is Frank's closest approach to a conventional travel book and one of his most relaxed pieces of writing.

I *The Great Experiment*

As Frank prowls around Russia he is a perceptive but sympathetic observer. He wants to believe that the Soviets have formed a corrective for social chaos, but his Yankee scepticism and reserve nourish his doubts. He alternately glows and frets. He resolves to be ruthless in his scrutiny of the Russian people, but he is charmed at the outset by their good will. He eludes his interpreter and his Russian hosts to wander in the maze of gloomy streets in Leningrad. Or he frustrates the interpreter by dragging him to the old Petersburg of Dostoevsky instead of visiting the new factories and schools. He goes to a Soviet court and feels that it is the first court of human justice he has ever known. Excitedly, he pulls the protesting interpreter into another courtroom in the building in which a woman judge solves a difficult paternity case on practical rather than on moral grounds. But, when he reaches a huge factory kitchen full of guzzling "collective creatures," Frank confesses that his training makes him "wonder if the old worker's table in his private kitchen with his family alone around him was not more human."

The high point of the book is reached, however, not in the cities but on the river. Frank floats down the Volga like a middle-aged Huck Finn who is "poised between two worlds"—Europe and Asia—and is awed by the paradox of Russia as exemplified in the peasants. "For these people are beasts; and yet a human pity, exquisite in grace, luminous in understanding, shines within them. These are men and women: yet their deeds do nothing to lift them above their cattle." They wait like dumb cattle on the wharf for the steamer; some have been waiting all day, others a day and two nights.

Time and comfort mean no more to these humans than to the horses: ". . . . Before a high wood grille are half a thousand muzhiks. Men lie on their backs, heads on hard bundles: . . . Mothers, with boiling samovars before them, have laid their children to sleep on rugs or on the naked stone. Some have stretched out and placed their babes on their breasts. In the arms of some women lie their husbands, . . . Children weave in and out of the thick throng, a crust of bread in one hand while the other touches the grime and filth of their passage." After twelve more hours of waiting, the *Raskolnikov* finally arrives just before dawn. Then an incredible scene takes place, one repeated at every subsequent docking on the Volga:

> The entire throng tried to board the narrow gangplank at once. It had waited twenty——thirty——forty hours: it could not wait another instant! Women with bundles were thrown down and trodden; . . . Men, gray-bearded, leaped on the shoulders of the mob before them and tried to climb the tangle of protesting heads; youths dug down into the knot of legs and skirts, pushed their way subterraneously forward. And rose a symphony of shouts, howls, oaths, objurgations, grunts and squeals, while the flimsy gangway groaned. . . .
>
> . . . when the huge muzhik body was spread safe along the lower deck, sweating and steaming among the kitchens, the steerage and latrines, the sailors scratched a cool ear and drew in the plank. We started down the Volga.

Frank correctly sees these village-bound peasants as a major problem for revolutionary Russia. The organic pulse of the city workers will have to be strong enough to transfigure these simple children of the soil if revolutionary Russia is to become an organic body and survive.

In Moscow, a great electric plant fills him with elation, for he believes that the workers—twenty-five thousand of them—are happy, are whole men and women working together to create a world. Nevertheless, he admits that the corruption of personal power may find its way into industrial management as there are signs of it already in the political world: "A new falsehood, as hideous as ours, may make havoc in this world." After talking with the Russian intellectuals, he wonders if there is "not danger that the Communist truth take an accessible form which is *half-truth?* that the half-truth harden into a lie? that a new formal falsehood stifle Russia?"

In the last section of the book, "Meditation on the Atlantic," Frank ruminates on the questions that his Russian trip has raised. His gravest concern is that the Marxist mood, "were it to harden into an effective creed, with its exclusive stress on *social* progress and its neglect of the *personal* value, would indubitably prevent the flowering of true persons: . . ." He decries the slide into dogma reflected in the sanctity of the official party line, the evolving police state, and the paradoxical emulation of capitalism. Naturally, he rejects dialectical materialism as a philosophy for a new world culture; but he believes that it is a legacy of history and will change as the Revolution evolves.

Meanwhile, all must keep open minds and work for "the most precious social event, the most precious social life, of our crucial epoch": "Every man and woman who is unwilling that human life should be a mere bog of personal lusts, who lays claim to belief in those values which men have lived for in all ages, under such names as God and truth and beauty, owes loyalty to Russia. Russia is our time's most conspicuous stronghold in the country of the human spirit. We must defend the Soviet Union with our spirit; if need be, we must defend it with our bodies."

The American tourist thus becomes a fellow traveler! *Dawn In Russia* suggests how the intellectuals of the early 1930's began to see and to feel about Russia. It marks Frank's plunge into the crusade, but it also reveals what is too often overlooked in retrospect: his commitment is inspired by hope for a better world and qualified by his doubts about the Marxist way. The quoted passage is a glowing expression of the inspiration, but it is followed by this significant reservation: "The American intellectual above all must beware of a false emulation, which in accepting the letter destroys the spirit. We must be loyal to the social aims of Russia; . . . But above all, we must be loyal—like the men of

Russia—to our own needs and intuitions. We must forge our part of the world future in the form of our own genius."

Thus *Dawn in Russia*, though a dated book, is interesting because it pictures a now forgotten, even unknown, Russia and offers thereby a useful perspective on the present. In addition, it affords a glimpse of the psychology of one writer of the 1930's who became a supporter of Communism and thereby an example of a phenomenon which has baffled Un-American Activities Committees ever since. Anyone who wants to understand Frank's subsequent activities as a spokesman for the political left should start with this book.

II *Social Action*

Waldo Frank's romance with Communism was intense but short-lived, dramatic but anti-climactic. Unlike many other fellow travelers of the period, Frank's approach to Communism is intellectual rather than emotional, critically analytical rather than doctrinaire. Although *Dawn in Russia* contains Frank's first formal critique of Marx, he had expressed some of its ideas earlier. The words of an interview in Lima in 1929 clearly define his position during the 1930's:

> I am not an opponent of Communism . . . ; nor am I a Communist. . . . A merely political revolution and a merely economic revolution are only partial transformations. From this point of view my communism is deeper, goes down much farther; it does not stay on the surface as has remained—for lack of new men, new ideas, new spirit—the experiment made in Russia. The revolution that I desire must be total and must begin with the transformation of men. Such a movement can come only from within, from the very depths of the human spirit.[2]

Frank's intellectual approach, however, did not preclude a political phase in his career marked by extensive polemical journalism and intensive social action. In August, 1929, he joined a writer's committee of thirty, headed by Sherwood Anderson, Fannie Hurst, and Theodore Dreiser, which attempted to raise money for Southern textile workers on strike since May. During 1930, he wrote some propaganda pamphlets for Latin American radicals. Upon his return from the tour of Russia, Frank spoke to some two thousand Friends of the Soviet Union, joined a group of American writers protesting persecution of Chinese authors by their government, and then in February, 1932, headed the Independent Miners' Relief Committee in Harlan County, Kentucky, with truck loads of food for the striking coal miners. Vigilantes overturned the trucks, escorted his group to the state line, and roughed Frank up. The episode led to a congressional hearing at which Frank testified.[3] In July, *Dawn In Russia* was published, parts of it having appeared serially in periodicals during October and November of the previous year.

In August, Frank returned to Washington as head of a delegation of writers from the National Committee for the Defense of Political Prisoners seeking an audience with President Hoover to protest the treatment of the Bonus Army. Hoover refused to receive the delegation. Frank drew up his revolutionary manifesto, which calls upon the intellectuals to desert the middle class and to join "the proletarians and farmers" in the class war; and he published it in the September *New Masses.* The fifth section of the tract reveals his motivation and mood: "The world is in crisis. Men and women are starving; they are being demoralized by unemployment; when they attempt even to protest they are being bludgeoned back to slavery by the armed mobs of Business fascism. At such a time, I cannot forever remain in my library, although my essential work lies there. I must from time to time make clear, in language simpler than the language of my books——in the language of physical comradeship——my solidarity with the people."[4] He follows the manifesto with a public endorsement of the Communist Party's presidential ticket of Browder and Ford.

This political activity did not, however, keep Frank out of the library; the long gestation period of the new novel was almost at an end. In the month of publication of *Dawn In Russia*, he revised the Onís translation of Güiraldes' *Don Segundo Sombra;* by September, he was started on a draft of the novel and completed Part One–forty-five thousand words–by the end of the month. Then he struggled for over a year to bring the long narrative into being. For two weeks in October, 1933, he lectured in Pennsylvania and visited the depressing coal-mining towns. His literary and social interests were now one, as the novel shows, and he jotted in Notebook XI the implications of this union: ". . . perhaps the important steps are three: 1. Conviction, matured & reconsidered, that I am a novelist——& must write stories. 2. Conviction, ditto, that I am a communist. 3. Conviction, ditto, that I believe in God. The synthesis of these three convictions is the life of the novel . . . and probably will be the life and form of all I ever write."

The synthesis did not come easily. In November, Frank sailed for South America, hopeful that a change of scene would help him with the novel. The strategem worked; when, after three months in Chile and Argentina, he returned to New York, the book was almost complete and he was already thinking of its sequel, or a story of Alma's life, or of his father's. He handed *The Death and Birth of David Markand* to Maxwell Perkins on April 30, worked on proof until the middle of August, and near the end of the month visited the Alton Bay and Manchester areas of New England where Alma had spent her girlhood. After closely studying her family, Frank decided to defer the story of Markand and to write *The Second Coming*, which he sketched in Notebook XI as "the saga of the Girl who, (like Alma) rises from Protestant America with the true religion . . . . this girl should become the woman whom Markand finally meets & with whom he finds fulfillment—as does she with him. This would mean that her saga is II of the whole Markand Series: and III their coming together and mature fulfillment & of the American Word through them."

In September Frank made two important field trips to the scenes of the great textile strike which had begun at Fall River and spread to Providence, Pawtucket, and other mill towns. His article on the strike appeared in *New Masses*; and he gave a series of twelve lectures in Boston, New York, Wilkes-Barre, and Chicago to labor groups. On October 8, 1934, *The Death and Birth of David Markand* was published; by October 28, Frank sadly recorded in his journal that his novel had been "stopped" by unfavorable reviews. His return to fiction was a failure.

III *Markand*

The Death and Birth of David Markand is not a failure even if, like many novels, it is not an unqualified success. In it, as in all of his fiction, Frank experiments with form and theme with mixed results. When he wrote the fifty-thousand-word draft of the work in 1927 at St. Georges d'Oléron, he entitled it *The Birth of David Markand* and envisioned it as a sequel to *The Dark Mother* but as one written in the style of the lyric novels. By January, 1929, however, the work had acquired "a whole new dimension," as the following entry in Notebook X makes clear:

> And the unilateral "portrait" form of the book as a whole has been abandoned. The aesthetic structure of the novel will be radically different from what I had supposed. The surface form,

so successful in Rahab and in many City Block stories, is no longer valid for what I feel. More profoundly the novel will be
an organic creation of America 1.
whence emerges a Man 2.
whence is posited (at the end) 3.
the fertile junction (or, at least, the moving toward each other in attraction) of this Man and this America.

But Frank had to experience firsthand more of this America before the novel could become an organic creation of it. "I am on the point of a brief visit to the mines of Kentucky in the great strike," he wrote in his notebook. "I expect, primarily, to win of this, the renewed taste of America." That brief visit and the other social involvements of the years between 1929 and 1932 gave him that "renewed taste" and the new dimension for the novel. By abandoning "the unilateral 'portrait' form" of the lyric novels, which concentrated on the person and his "ecstasy," he enlarged the structure of his narrative to include social action and to create a consciousness of life as a whole in what he later called a "symphonic" form, because it, like the cultural histories, develops themes in counterpoint.

In *The Death and Birth of David Markand*, for example, the themes associated with the protagonist are supposed to develop contrapuntally to those representing America so that David becomes "the symbol for the American world striving to be born. . . ."[5] The fact that the symphonic whole is not fully realized is in part attributable to Frank's inability to reject completely the "unilateral 'portrait' form." Thus, as Bittner points out, "the unilateral shows through too often," especially in the first two sections of the novel which are too much in the form of *The Dark Mother* to permit effective integration of the themes of David and of America.[6] In these sections, David's actions are not clearly or consistently motivated in terms of his quest; and the interaction of his life and of society is blurred or obscured.

In Book One, "Deane and Company," the David Markand of *The Dark Mother* is portrayed as the passive result of the combined influences of the Helen Daindrie whom he married at the close of *The Dark Mother* and of the business career his uncle created for him. He has family, friends, fortune; but he is mysteriously troubled and restless: "all the familiar is strange. It has been growing on him through the winter, this daily experience of waking as of being born into strangeness."[7] He feels vaguely dissatisfied with his lot. He lives in a home created for him by his father-in-law and decorated by his wife. The profitable merger of Deane and Company with United Tobacco Industries, which he and Anthony Deane had hoped would not take place, has made him a mere executive cog in the now impersonal business mechanism. Recently, his wife has been rising very early to go alone on some secret mission. Even his son, Tony, is no bridge between the worlds of the familiar and the strange; the two worlds exclude each other.

As David sits at the breakfast table with his son and daughter, he scans the headlines of his morning paper. The problems and follies of the world make him think only of the irony of his self-sufficient, easy existence; and his mind wanders back into the world of *The Dark Mother*: to Tom Rennard, the sinner who tried to possess him; to the maid Ann, who had satisfied his passion; and to his cousin Lois, his first love. This world and its David Markand must die before a new David can be born into the world in the headlines. One of these, for example, speaks of strike violence in New Jersey and of the jailing of Paul Wood, a labor leader. By the end of the novel, the reborn David Markand knows and suffers for that same Paul Wood.

At the reading of Anthony Deane's will, David learns that he is now a rich man and therefore free to indulge in a quest of himself, if he chooses. His perceptive uncle, having foreseen that David might want to leave the business, has pointed one way for him to start by leaving to him the house in Clearden, Connecticut, that had belonged to David's mother. But his discontent is still amorphous and his rebellion quixotic. After the reading of the will, he drifts into sexual intercourse with Lois, for whom he had felt physical attraction in the previous novel; but he discovers that his passion is locked wholly within himself and that he has again been selfish in receiving all while giving nothing. In a later scene he picks up a showgirl, only to find that he has no desire for a sexual encounter; so he gives her a hundred dollars and departs. The implication that he is incapable of a normal sexual relationship before his "birth" is underscored in his last union with Helen: "and they lay deep in an ecstasy timeless and climaxless. His own body had grown impersonal, he had died from it, his being with Helen had been a bleeding away."

David's discontent and doubt are now intensified by Helen's resolution of her need "to feel and to enact a part in a universal world," a need which, "under whatever name, is of religion." When she tells David that she has "found the Truth" by joining the Catholic Church, he is crushed by his sense of remoteness: "She was whole, and he for the first time outside her. He felt himself crumbling. . . ." He blames himself for Helen's action—she had been "made desperate by some lack in him"—and he decides that he must go in search of himself: he must no longer live in ignorance of the meaning of life while passively taking that ignorance for granted. The key "lay somewhere, silently, within him. . . . In a silence far remote from his wife and children." He looks up his old friend Tom Rennard, whom he has not seen since their break, twelve years before; gives him the management of his estate; and leaves for his boyhood home in Clearden.

In Book Two—"The Mothers"—David starts his quest appropriately at his birthplace, where he finds a substitute mother and lover in Deborah Gore, a widow who cooks for him. Trying to find himself in his heritage, David reads his father's papers, finds his father's letters full of unhappiness, his mother's matter-of-factly devoted. In an obviously symbolic action, Markand sweats over a garden, kneeling—as Helen is probably kneeling "at some Roman altar"—to plant the seed in the earth's darkness. His neighbor Stan Poldiewicz, a Polish immigrant farmer who tried to be a chef in Kansas, and his wife Christine, whom he had taken from a Kansas farm, give him a glimpse of living as an act of love. Although David draws from his past only a dark world, there are within it mysterious Presences, of which one is the form of his mother speaking with the voice of his father. A poetic passage, like one of those in *Holiday*, chants that David's move to the city "was his young dying," that he had no life there even with his family, and that he "will have no being/. . . . Until desire is born within" him.

David is too depressed and homesick, however, to respond to the Presences. He decides to return home; but Deborah Gore, who believes that a visitation from an Angel has made it possible for her to endure her harsh, cruel life, insists that he is not ready to go home; he must not ask his family to shape his life but must ask God to make what he wants. Unable to believe in God or in himself, David remains in Clearden—although Tom Rennard appears to urge his return in view of Helen's pregnancy—because he feels that he has discovered a reality in his togetherness with Deborah Gore which, if denied, would reduce everything at once to chaos.

Since David is still struggling with his passivity in "The Mothers," social problems are barely evident in this section. Stan voices some criticism of a blind materialism which enslaves the peasants in Poland and shatters his vision of America: "All you Americans are wrong. All you see is facts, and facts is nothing. . . . You Americans . . . you say, we'll study them all separate, fact by fact, and know all about them. Well, you do that and you learn nothing. They ain't separate at all. They all joined together." When Lucy Demarest, "at loose ends in a life that bores her," fails to seduce David and acts with Deborah's son to have him run out of Clearden, the nasty, hypocritical small-town mind is revealed in a characteristic mob. As he and Deborah slip away in the darkness, David, humbly and sadly, prays—"he knows not to what Force joining him to these men"—for understanding: "let me learn why I have drawn their hate, how I can draw their love. For we are not separate: it is a lie, our separation, equal in us both."

Book Three—"The River"—carries David into the world of social conflict. Panoramic in scope, this section is divided into five parts: "The Prairie," "Helen," "Pastoral," "The City," and "The Gulf." In "The Prairie," David and Deborah drift westward through Chicago to Centralia, Kansas. Between trains in New York, he telephones Rennard but not Helen, which is the kind of behavior that finally makes him an unbelievable character in the novel. In Centralia, Deborah, after suffering symbolically the pangs of childbirth, leaves David, her "true child . . . destined to be born a man," to find himself while she returns to her son, "who can never be wholly free of her flesh." David, in turn, comes to an understanding of the symbolic truth in Deborah's love and gives up his son, Tony: "In bringing him to Kansas, she had helped destroy his share in the world of Tony." Word of Tony's death from meningitis merely confirms, therefore, the symbolic rejection; but Markand's decision not to return home is not symbolic, as will be seen, and contributes to the unreality of his characterization.

The unreality is intensified by Frank's attempts to suggest David's arrested emotional and spiritual condition in symbolic sexual activities. First he rejects Irene, an aggressive young whore, all the while wondering if Deborah's God is responsible for his revulsion. Later he gets in bed with Irene but is interested only in seeing if he can shatter her passivity and make her feel. He indulges his egocentric will as if he hopes, by arousing Irene, to bring himself alive. Desire is yet to be born within him.

David's political development, the main theme of "The River," is more plausible than his emotional growth but still amorphous and tentative in "The Prairie." In his first small job as a freight handler, he experiences the petty grafting of foremen who demand kickbacks for employment. As a bartender in an illegal saloon, he learns that shady business is more interesting than his former work and "truer," since there are no hypocritical pretenses. When he hears that Tony is dead, he goes to the local bank to borrow money on his real name to return to New York; but then he discovers that the powerful banker is also the Big Boss of the liquor and prostitution rackets in Kansas, and the evil that he has been trying to ignore engulfs him. Disgust routs his despair, and he decides that he cannot go back to his way of life. His letter to Helen projects metaphorically what lies ahead after he leaves "The River":

> I've got to go ahead, till the way ahead leads home. Maybe I have got to go through something like what you went through before you found your Church. Was it like a big mountain you had to climb alone? . . .
>
> . . . . But I have to go forward, even though it seems (and that is the worst of it) like going downward, more than like going up a mountain.

Almost broke, he takes poorer and poorer lodgings until, close to starvation, he accepts a handout from his Negro landlady, protesting, "You shouldn't feed me, . . . I'm your enemy. I got two hundred thousand dollars."

The social scene is broadened at this point by an interlude involving Stan Poldiewicz's misfortunes. Stan—unable to stay in Clearden after the mob had called his wife Christine a whore for marrying a Pole and for befriending David—tries to get work as a chef in New York, is kicked by a policeman's horse in a strike, and is then rejected as a dumb Polack by the Union. He dies, muttering "Man is bad"; and David has destroyed another loved one. Christine goes to her brother's in Melleville, where she will meet David at the close of "The Prairie."

David, in flight from the revealed evil of Centralia, meanwhile falls in with some IWW workers, meets Paul Wood, and discovers that these men are fighting violence with violence. When he realizes that he is carrying dynamite to blast a struck mine, he walks out, wondering which side he is really on. He wanders toward Philip Dwelling's home in Melleville, full of bewilderment and doubt before "the insane confusion of men against men." But he is hopeful that a view of the whole, instead of the isolated fragments, will disclose the true "orbit of this human cycle!"

The brief section called "Helen" pictures David's wife at confession, and her easily arrived at peace of mind is presented in counterpoint to David's struggles, which are then resumed in "Pastoral." In Kansas, David, like Waldo Frank many years before, works on a local paper, goes to the national convention of the Farmer's Guild, and discovers how the small farmers are betrayed by their leaders. But he sees in this betrayal the evidence of general greed and lust for power: "the Guild's got the same aims as Wall Street. You're nothing but a bunch of small-money men getting mad at the big-money men and snarling for more profit." David works out a law of life which suggests his motivation and objective: "Live for power, in terms of fame or money, and you stink. . . . Try to live without power, and you die. . . . There's something more to this 'law' . . . a third clause we haven't got hold of." Hester Dwelling, hungry for power and fearful of David's growing influence, forces him to leave; and he heads for Chicago to meet Helen.

In "The City," Markand experiences his moment of symbolic death and birth. He tells Helen that he must continue to run from her since she represents a world that he must escape. He gets work in a packing house and lives in the shabby home of a young Mexican fellow worker, Juan Fierro. Drugged by toil, David slumbers like a foetus, "removed by sleep from the world of Markand" and lulled by "the dark womb joy of the workers!" But all the past of Markand sets up a bitter conflict, and he falls into a delirium in which his two selves do battle. Juan brings a priest, and David, hurling a glass of water at him, shouts, "Not the priest. Not Helen! . . . I won't waken with you." Like a sick child, he clasps Juan's wife, seeking her breast. When Juan tells Marita to give David whatever he needs, she gives him her breast, an obvious symbol of birth.

Like the newborn infant, however, David develops slowly. Theodora Lench, the wife of a fawning meat packer whom Markand had met at literary gatherings when he had first arrived in Chicago, takes him to her retreat in the Wisconsin woods. He talks little, swims alone, has no interest in her world of art, books, and ideas. When he says that he has been falling like a river and that all rivers should flow south, Theodora decides to remold him, to educate him in her world; she takes him to a Montessori School in Alabama which she supports.

In "The Gulf," Theodora fails to make David over in her image because he soon discovers that she represents his old life disguised in a new form. With this discovery he finally realizes why he had left his home and why he must reject those who would capture him. He tries to explain to Theodora: " 'I cannot stand this world I've been in, all my life, and Helen is in, and we are in! . . . I can't love you in it, I cannot separate you or me enough from it, to keep from hating us both for being still in it. I haven't had the guts to get out, which means to seek another world.' " She leaves him for Hollywood; and Lida Sharon, a radical young Jewish teacher at the school, redirects his education by having him read Marx.

"The River" having reached "The Gulf," the last section of the novel then turns to "The Mountain" and the education of David through social conflict. Its effective counterpoint is introduced in a series of short scenes of simultaneous action. In her home with baby Barbara, Helen turns from newspaper headlines of munitions, strikes, and profits to a letter from David. Around the corner from her house, a young Socialist organizer, John Byrne, reads a letter from comrade Paul Wood urging him to go south: "If we can get the IWW ideology into their heads before the mills bust their nerve, we'll start the revolution down there." In Hollywood, Theodora Lenck commits suicide; in Louisiana, Lida Sharon sends Byrne an invitation to visit. When Byrne does visit the school, David, shaken by Theodora's death, leaves with him. They hike through Alabama, doing odd jobs for food and sleeping in barns. An idealistic and religious farm girl, Jane Priest, joins them to escape her incestuous father. Atheistic Byrne falls in love with her, and David follows them farther away from the world of "rational Rennard, the rational-religious Helen!" An Appalachian mountain symbolizes for David the barrier between himself and his life: "The mountain was huge . . . because it was the Pass of his destiny, and its bowels the fire in which all that David Markand had been, and dreamed to be, must die ere he transcend it."

The trio eventually moves into Kentucky to persuade the striking coal miners to join the IWW instead of the United Miners and to work toward socialization of mining and opposition to war. The scenes are vividly and dramatically developed, largely because Frank had made the trip to Harlan County; and

David receives rough treatment similar to Frank's while Jane and Byrne are murdered. As David lies unconscious, the narrative shifts abruptly to Tom Rennard, who is arriving in Washington to represent the steel company in which he has invested David's money. Having made David a fortune, Rennard decides to sell the steel stock since Helen will object to making money out of munitions. Tom hopes that the money will bind David to his world, just as money has joylessly bound him.

Upon regaining consciousness, David, who has finally decided to return home, starts for Washington where he has arranged to meet Rennard. Although not yet the whole Person, Markand has, nevertheless, moved toward completeness, as his thoughts reveal: "Everything had changed. He no longer needed to die. . . . He saw everything salient, near and new. . . . He had never come so near to human beings: not to Helen . . . not to his children, not to his mother. . . . The world was an organic and palpable closeness, and he walked motionless behind it, . . ." But he believes that it has now been revealed to him that passive acceptance of the world is death and that the world he began trying to cast off four years before is his dead body from which he must free himself if he is to be born again. He returns to the graves of John Byrne and Jane Priest to see if he can understand their death in life in contrast to his. At the graves he thinks:

> —Your death was not unhappy, because you wholly lived, and even your death was of your life.
>
> —Your life, your feelings and thoughts and deeds, were all one: one body. That is health.
>
> —I envied you, knowing how different I am. I will no more envy you. I will be like you. I will do like you.
>
> —I have no body! My body was the world in which I lived, with Mother and with Helen. At last it is dead. . . But it sticks to me, . . .
>
> —I hear you. You say I have not killed it. While this dead body prevails in the world, I have not killed it within me. There must be a new, living body!
>
> . . . .
>
> —To live within a meek acceptance of all life, to say Yes to everything, to what one's blood hates, also is to die.
>
> . . . .
>
> —The whole? . . . It is before the deed of human life . . . what I saw in Tony's newborn eyes. And it is after the deed of human life . . . what I feel now to be you, beloved friends, who have lived truly.

—But for a man, the whole can only be its enactment in his act, its embodiment in his body. . . .

—And this is your meaning of class! The world of men is threatened with death, because the class of men who rule has died. There is a class, hardly born, which struggles with the world to live. By its struggle for life the whole world may be reborn alive again. By the life of this class, which is a part, the whole may live. . . .

—I embrace your class. All men who want to live today must embrace it . . . . the living body of the class which now is life.

Thus the search for God must lead to social action. It would have been an appropriate merger with which to end the novel, but Frank elects to subject David to a test of his decision to return home—a sordid melodramatic test which will make his embrace of class ambiguous and jarring. Having wandered from the Kentucky border to Washington, David starts for Tom's hotel; but the newsboys' cries of "War" send him striding aimlessly away from official Washington into the Negro settlement. He goes into a basement restaurant and orders a bowl of soup, although he has no money. Three Negroes attack him when he cannot pay, but the huge Negress who owns the place will accept sexual intercourse in payment. Markand tries to make her world his—"He lusted for himself a body of life like hers, he who was bodiless. It would be peace, and he was tired"—but nausea grips him and he vomits. "Now Markand knew that he had taken the unpaid meal as a rite; a 'First Supper' it was to be of his newborn body." He had been unbearably ashamed when he had accepted food from the Negro in Kansas; "Now, he had rejoiced in his lack of shame; in his feeling of the right . . . he of the same class! . . . to take it. But he had vomited the ceremonial food. . . ."

The instinctive world of the Negress was not his; his seeking an escape to the peace of her world was just another way to die, not a new birth. He must first destroy the body of his living death if he is to be born again to a new life. His body begins to shudder in token of his awakening will: "The shudder in his body, he knew, was only a beginning. The shudder must grow . . . must rage, within the body of the world. . . . It must grind down the grinding institutions, it must turn the tide of men streaming to death back to their source, which is life." Markand had left his family because their lives were encompassed in this enemy Body that must be destroyed. He had needed to go from them to find the pass through the mountain and the strength to follow it. Having found the strength in the world of his martyred comrades, he can—and must—return to his loved ones to save them.

Thus *The Death and Birth of David Markand* represents a modern quest for salvation in a decadent world. Salvation for the individual lies in the discovery of God in the enigmatic diversity of life and in social action. Individual salvation—the development of the whole Person—must precede any attempt to revitalize the social body: "David learns that to assert his own egoistic will to power is the way of death, that when he acts selfishly, he can inflict only pain and suffering on others. To be reborn in the way of life-fulfillment he must accept his role within the organic Whole, must recognize he is indissolubly linked with his fellow men, so that his own salvation and freedom lie in acting as his brother's keeper."[8]

Unfortunately, David, despite the laudable theme, is stillborn in the narrative. Although his complex psychological frustration is recognizable and understandable, he never becomes a plausible, moving expression of it. His passivity infects the reader until he becomes indifferent to the implications of David's bewilderment and impatient with the symbolic complexity of his actions, especially his ambiguous sexual encounters, which tend to mystify rather than illumine. The failure of these scenes is attributable for the most part to Frank's Naturalistic handling of sex for symbolic purposes, a technique which created difficulties for the readers of *City Block* and *Rahab* and which proves troublesome in all of his fiction. The symbolic import of David's sexual experiences, for example, is relatively clear; but the Naturalistic handling of those experiences clashes with their mystical implications in such a way as to make David increasingly implausible as a character.

The failure of method in this context is symptomatic of the weakness, if not failure, of Frank's symphonic novels as wholes. The Naturalistic treatment of experience does not blend with the mystical concept of reality in a harmonious contrapuntal development of themes, and the reader is disturbed, if not repulsed, by the dissonances. The mysticism is perhaps the more discordant element since the modern temper has created an unresponsive audience for it. With such an audience, the effect of the Naturalistic style is to intensify hostility to the mystical, for the style leads readers to expect resolutions within that frame of reference. Conversely, the readers who accept mystical experiences are apt to be distressed or offended by Naturalistic details.

CHAPTER 7

Revolutionary Writer

DESPITE the negative reaction to *The Death and Birth of David Markand*, Frank continued to work on the scenario for *The Second Coming* during the fall of 1934 while he was completing a series of six lectures at the New School. A projected lecture tour had to be cancelled, however, for lack of engagements; his increasing political activity was reducing his audience. He was co-editor and author of one chapter of *America and Alfred Stieglitz*, published in December. Late in the month he returned to South America, visiting Argentina and Chile. As a member of the International Committee for the Defense of Political Prisoners, which had protested the treatment of the bonus marchers in 1932, Frank filed in 1935 his personal minority statement against the mass executions in Russia. He also signed a call for an American Writers' Congress. In March, when he spent two weeks in New Hampshire gathering material for the new novel, he lived in one of the corporation houses of a textile mill in Manchester in order to experience firsthand the desolation of industrial life.

While he was visting Concord, he attended a meeting of the local Communist party and addressed a radical union of Swedish granite cutters. He called on active fellow travelers in New England and then swung down to the Wilkes-Barre and Scranton areas. On May 23 he delivered a major address—"Values of the Revolutionary Writer"—at the opening session of the American Writers' Congress and was elected by acclamation chairman of the permanent organization, the League of American Writers. In June he went to Paris in response to insistent cables from Gorki, Gide, Rolland, Aragon, and Malraux, urging him to be the American delegate to the International Congress of Writers for the Defense of Culture. At the Congress he addressed an audience of three thousand on "The Writer's Essential Duty."

Upon his return to his summer home in Truro, Massachusetts, Frank tried to start again on his novel without success. In November, he wandered to Savannah, Georgia, to see if a change of scene would help. Although he had not even started on a draft of the book, he began thinking of its successor, the novel which would unite Mark and Mary in, according to an entry in Notebook XII, "the Poem of the emergence of communist society in *full human experience* . . . . the transfiguration of the Meaning of God into terms of modern man and woman, and of the Communist Society." Plans for this third volume evidently unlocked his creative force, for he immediately began his first draft of *The Second Coming* and completed Book I by the end of December. He worked steadily and effectively throughout 1936 until the election campaign called him back to political matters.

In May, he had resigned his chairmanship of the League of American Writers in order to devote his time and energy to the novel, but in September he became an active member of the Committee of Professional Groups for Browder and Ford; he then joined Browder on his campaign tour, ostensibly as a reporter for the *Daily Worker.* He filed about a dozen news stories on political rallies in Youngstown, Pittsburgh, Chicago, Milwaukee, and Terre Haute, all stressing the fine spirit of the gatherings. On September 30, he was one of the four members of the campaign party jailed with Browder in Terre Haute, Indiana, to prevent a meeting there; he wrote a mocking account of his experience in an essay, "Terre Haute Hotel." The publicity resulting from this affair led to Frank's becoming the main speaker at a Communist rally in New York's Town Hall on October 4.

In November, Frank accompanied Browder to Tampa and Detroit; but he was becoming increasingly concerned over the fate of the Spanish Loyalists, and he went to work in their behalf. He visited Washington, addressed the Progressive Educational Association of New York on "Social Philosophy and the Arts," and in December became the head of the American Society for Technical Aid to Spanish Democracy.

In January, 1937, Frank was the chief American delegate and the guest of honor at the Congress of Writers and Artists in Mexico City. At the opening session he delivered an address, "The Artist: Minister of Freedom." He remained in Mexico until March, busy with the work of the Congress, with interviews—including two long sessions with Leon Trotsky—and with impromptu speeches, especially before the crowds of students who welcomed him wherever he appeared. He also became the official guest of the provincial government of Jalisco. Despite all this activity, he somehow found the time to finish the first typed version of the first two books of the novel and to check the proofs of a new collection of essays to be called *In the American Jungle.* The collection was published in April upon his return to New York.

I *The Jungle*

Harold Clurman, a director of the Group Theater, was responsible for the general idea and organization of *In the American Jungle.* From the articles Frank had published between 1925 and 1936 in periodicals in the United States and all over the world—among them *The Adelphi* (London), *Europe* (Paris), *La Nacion* (Buenos Aires), *Occidente* (Rome)—Clurman selected those which would create a kind of "collective portrait" of the Boom, the Depression, and the Social Revolution. Thus the section entitled "Boom Year Sketches" includes the individual essays containing the biographical material used earlier in this study and brief pieces on such characteristic pursuits of the late 1920's as baseball at the Polo Grounds, the Dempsey-Tunney fight in Philadelphia, the new gold rush to Florida, and gangster murders.

"Portraits" identifies a group of profiles—Randolph Bourne, Charles Chaplin, D. H. Lawrence, Herbert Croly, Sigmund Freud, Sherwood Anderson, and Hart Crane; satiric descriptions of American culture—movies, the "comedy of commerce," and jazz; and attacks on American ideas as expressed in pseudo literature and in utilitarian art. Section Three discusses, mostly in the form of book reviews, writers from Poe and Thoreau to Lewis Mumford, Oswald Spengler, and T. S. Eliot. The selections comprising "Some Practical Conclusions for the Survival of Man" are derived from Frank's addresses to the First United States Congress Against War, the American Writers' Congress, and the International Congress of Writers.

The diversity and scope of subject matter in this collection is matched by the variety and adaptability of Frank's prose style. Yet there is a kind of over-all unity created by his characteristic point of view. Everybody and everything are entrapped in the American jungle, which is, in the words of the quotation Frank uses from *The Re-discovery of America,* "rich in denatured elements of a transplanted world."[1] Ball player or artist is equally betrayed by the mechanization of the spirit in American culture. Frank's tone may be lightly satirical as in "Murder As Bad Art" or "Terre Haute Hotel"; it may become caustic in naming Mencken "King of the Philistines" or hortatory in the speeches to revolutionary writers; but his theme is always the same: only the whole person, the "man who *knows*, by immediate experience, the organic continuity of his self with the cosmos," can escape the jungle of materialism. The true Person is, like D. H. Lawrence, "no dupe of the parade of detailed separatenesses that clutter mortal eye." The Person does not share the American superstition that motion is progress; his metaphysical consciousness makes him master of the machines and of his machine-dominated culture. The revolutionary task that challenges human life is "the recreating of language, of society and of man in the image of the Whole which is God. . . ."

The revolutionary scope of the task, intensified by the obvious need everywhere for true social justice, pushes Frank logically toward Marxism; but he confounds the doctrinaire Marxists by coupling Spinoza with Marx: "every man who wants to *enact* social justice in the modern world must be a Marxist in spirit although he may reject certain Marxist dogmas." Marx has a workable program for achieving economic justice in an industrial society; Spinoza "has best established the organic being of God *in* matter and in human thought; . . . has made rational the ancient mystic intuition that the cosmic dwells within the man in so far as the man grows self-conscious." Accordingly, Frank warns the revolutionary writer that he must not be just a "fellow traveler"; for "only by deepening his comprehension of cultural historic forms, such as religion, in which . . . man's profoundest intuitions of his organic nature were embodied, can the writer touch the *spirit* of the American worker and farmer and middle class, to release their spirit from obsolete forms into new creative channels. And only thus can we save them from the decayed devotions which are the treacherous bait of the fascists."

Such sentiments could not be tolerated indefinitely by American Communists. The break came within a month after the publication of *In the American Jungle*; and the immediate cause was Frank's letter in the *New Republic* on May 12, 1937, recommending the establishment of an international tribunal to inquire into the Soviet case against Trotsky.[2] Earl Browder replied with an abusive letter in the *New Masses*, and Frank's period of "fellow traveling" ended, although not his interest in Marxism or the Russian revolution. He even contemplated starting a magazine in an effort to bring some depth and character to the movement, but he soon became too busy with his new novel to give time to this project.[3]

He completed his revisions of *The Second Coming* near the end of July. When Maxwell Perkins rejected the novel, Frank broke his contract with Scribner's and sailed for England. The Spanish War was in his mind, and he felt an obligation to go to Spain. But he procrastinated while working "furiously" for four months rewriting the novel. Then he went to Spain for three weeks as a "Guest of the Government." He was welcomed by writers and soldiers in Madrid and "at the front," but Browder's denunciation had created difficulties. An official party paper attacked Frank as a Trotskyite on its front page, but the Spanish government remained discreetly silent. Individual Spanish Communists were friendly and sympathetic but refused to risk offending Moscow by speaking out for Frank. He left Madrid convinced, as he revealed in his notebook, that Russia was a menace to the "sweetness of individual communists." Meanwhile, his novel had been rejected by nine American publishers; nevertheless, an English house, Gollancz, accepted it; and *The Bridegroom Cometh* was published in London on October 24, 1938. Doubleday issued an American edition in May of the next year.

II *The World of Mary Donald*

In *The Death and Birth of David Markand* the chaotic forces of the universe act upon the immature organism of the man, David, bringing death to the old forms of his being and potential birth of the new forms. In *The Bridegroom Cometh* the universe is felt and experienced through the sensibility and will of a woman, Mary Donald, whose evolving consciousness shapes the structure of the novel. As she matures, Mary forms her universe by the dimensions of her acts of joy, adjustment, and survival. The dynamics of the former novel are realized in David's struggle for salvation through a readjustment to society, chiefly on the instinctive-intuitive level of action. In *The Bridegroom Cometh* the struggle is projected in terms of Mary's personal adjustment, chiefly on an emotional plane. "Mary is the woman," Frank wrote in Notebook XII, "who must find the wholeness of her actual world for Bridegroom, in order to give birth to her truth." Later, he added that *Behold the Lord Cometh*—one of his early titles for the book—"is, most essentially, the story . . . of the sad meeting of youth with the world its fathers and mothers have bequeathed it. And it is the story of youth's emergence to reject this world-inheritance, in favor of the spirit & tradition of America to create a new world."

This theme lends itself to the symphonic form Frank also uses in this novel. Mary Donald matures through personal attachments; each of the seven parts of the narrative centers upon some crisis in Mary's life as she searches for love in a society which responds only to power. The musical parallel is underscored by using the notes in the scale as titles for each section of the story. Thus "Do" portrays Mary's first problem with love because of her inability to effect a meaningful relationship with her father or her stepmother. This failure in turn inspires her passionate, adolescent devotion to Christ and to his minister, Mr. Lamy. The novel opens with the dramatic scene of Mary's baptism in a river in New England on the day World War I breaks out in Europe. Mary is only fifteen; and, as she awaits her turn to enter the water, her mind slides easily and naturally into flashbacks of the events and relationships leading up to this high point in her religious fundamentalism. Various themes are heard briefly and then dropped, as in a musical composition. A Saturday night bath with her twin, Martha, becomes a moving vignette of the hard piety of her bleak home: the cowed, ineffective father living only for the Second Coming; the frustrated, bitter stepmother hating the man who has failed to give her a son and hating his two daughters "in piety of Christ's promise to give to those who hated this world a lovelier world."[4]

Mary's flashback moves to her own mother, to her grandmother, to Martha, to the first stirrings of sex, and to the conflict between her fundamentalist attitudes and her love of beauty. Frank continues to use the expressionistic techniques of the early novels, especially the interior monologue, to show how his heroine's actions are motivated almost wholly by her feelings; but expressionism is now balanced with realism, so that the conscious mind functions as well in dramatic scenes involving interesting characters.[5] Mrs. Gudgeon, who will make it possible for Mary to get to college despite parental opposition, is one such character, a memorable small-town eccentric.

Contrapuntally presented in "Do" is the threat of Armageddon; in "Re" Wilson declares war on the Central Powers. Mary is in her third year at Winant College, and a flashback traces her struggles to get there and some of her crucial experiences as a student. Her decision to go to college had been a tormenting one since she had believed that she was sinning in turning from

Christ to enter a school where dancing was permitted. Once in college, she gradually lost some of her more rigid fundamentalist beliefs, but she has become increasingly distressed by the sanctimonious hypocrisy of the students and teachers. The arguments about the war among the girls echo Frank's pacifist battles; and the students refer to various magazines, among them the *Seven Arts*, for support of their views. A radical young instructor in sociology, Doris Granes, gives an anti-war talk to the students, becomes interested in Mary, and leads her further from Christ. Mary forgets to pray for the first time, discovers the living world of nature, and decides to go to New York with Doris instead of finishing at Winant. A minor theme is Martha's total surrender to Sidney Harvard, another of Frank's satanic males. Martha, submissive but unstirred, is conscious only of the shadow of death.

"Mi" opens with a series of scenes which depict the simultaneous reactions to the news of the false Armistice by characters in a sweatshop, in the Stock Exchange, in City Hall, and in Harlem. In the subway, which is full of turmoil because of the news flash, Martha meets Sid; and flashbacks then reveal how and why they had both left the home town for New York: Sid to find the big, easy money; Martha to escape the loneliness of life without Sid. Mary hears the news at New Amsterdam College; and, when her classes are dismissed, she goes to the apartment of Doris Granes and her husband, Peter, where she has a room.

Now the experiences of the sisters are presented contrapuntally in a series of alternating scenes. To find her true self—the total Person—Mary continues, like David Markand, to shed her old way of life, to peel off layer by layer her fundamentalist outlook. She replaces Jesus with Doris Granes, discovering in this relationship a woman's need for fulfilling love. But Doris and Martha seek their fulfillment at the expense of wholeness, and so Mary becomes a kind of living rebuke to them. Doris's shallow husband, the adulterous yet possessive and jealous Peter, says of Mary, "That ignorant country kid sometimes makes me feel small!"

All around her are aware of a stubborn will in Mary, and Doris especially resents her goodness. The false Armistice symbolizes Mary's truce with Doris, but she continues to fight her and the fallen creatures around her. Mary thinks "of the worshipers at Loomis Lake shouting War on the World for peace, her father's frantic counting on the Prince of Peace while he let his wife make home a desert, a shambles of love." Mary fights free of her need for Doris when she discovers that Doris has a lover. In her resulting loneliness, she turns to Willem Taess, a wealthy, intellectual Dutch Jew.

Sid, now an active gangster, finally marries Martha; and Mary tries to find in their false world a peace without war. But ironically, while Mary works for the Parents' Aid Society, trying to find children for childless couples, Martha has an abortion. Mary's investigations of applicants for children lead her into the sordid world of toil and cruelty, which permits Frank to express his social criticism without doing violence to the story or to the characters. The world of children presents sharp, paradoxical contrasts to the world of adults. Mary's crises, like Markand's, arise from conflicts of the self and society, since Frank now sees mature self-awareness as attainable only through full social consciousness. But Mary's conflicts are more smoothly and functionally incorporated into the fiction than are Markand's, and Mary emerges as a more fully and richly realized character.

Mary accepts Willem only because he needs her; and in "Fa," the end of Part One, she tries to find love and herself through him. But first she must separate him from his morbid mother, symbol of the kind of living death the Person must escape. Meanwhile, Mary is also becoming aware of the class struggle and of the superficiality of the supposed intellectuals around her. She has already started to reject her soft, sleeping life with Taess when Sid disappears and Martha's crisis precipitates Mary's. Although destroyed by Sid's fate, Martha has at least known love; and, as Mary walks the desolate streets of a slum after leaving Martha, she hears a woman sobbing and, in her emotional state, sees her own whole life pass before her: "the long quest . . . for another Heaven, for another Jesus. . . ." And she concludes that her marriage is "a conspiracy for sleeping," which she must shatter if she is ever to awake. "The peace she has known and loved . . . Jesus, Willem . . . she knows is a sleep before life. She knows she was born to awake."

Mary's discovery marks the end of her beginning, which has the appropriately paradoxical title "The Last Days." In "Soh," the opening section of Part Two, entitled "The Second Coming," all of the old ties in her life are severed. She visits her girlhood home, only to realize that she is at last estranged not only from her parents' crabbed religious fundamentalism but also from her husband's equally sterile world. Her grandmother dies; and

Martha, who has joined Mary in their old home, drowns herself in the baptismal river when she hears that Sid has been murdered in a gang war. Willem comes to plead with Mary, but she ends their marriage, a decision symbolized in her intercourse with an old caretaker who "needed" to make love to a young woman.

A new way for Mary is discovered in this section at a Granes' party which brings a psychoanalyst, Philip Cariss, and a Bolshevik, Dolg, into her life. In presenting these characters Frank has an amusing time airing some of his pet theories about Shakespeare and Communism. Dolg's comments on the dramatist, which are drawn in part from a discussion of Shakespeare published in 1936 in *International Literature*, are in reality attacks on Britain and the party line. Cariss joins in the discussion as the author of a monograph on anal erotic symbolism in the Hamlet-Polonius exchange.[6] Dolg's long-winded exposition, however, also has a narrative function. His observation that "we live in a world without form, and . . . no longer know our chaos" helps Mary to recognize her problem: "Everything is separate. Jesus was up in the sky, separate . . . still is, though I don't believe. Truth was in an old Bible, speaking a separate tongue . . . no wonder I don't believe. That's what the human man meant. We're all to pieces." She realizes that loneliness is a condition of life and that she has been trying to live only in terms of her separatist will. Now she understands that her mind must assume direction of her will and bring about her total separation from her husband. "I do not love your life," she explains to him; "I am choking to death with loneliness, because it's not my world."

Mary tries in "La" to learn how to grow. Against the counter theme of the booming 1920's, expressed in a series of unrelated scenes of typical actions occurring simultaneously throughout the Western world, Mary sinks lower and lower in the economic scale as she tries to support herself. The shoddy, brutal prosperity of the postwar years is exposed in a flashback of Mary's sordid experiences as a worker. Eventually, she looks up Dolg as someone in a new, different kind of world who may be able to show her the way; and he places her in a collar factory as a Communist organizer. There a machine mutilates the hand of an employee, Lida Sharon, the radical teacher in the Montessori school in *The Death and Birth of David Markand.* When Mary visits the girl in the hospital, flashbacks reveal how the split in the Socialist movement led to the formation of the Communist party in the

United States. Other flashbacks show the problems of the bosses and sound the Marxist theme that the fault is not with the individual but with the system. Separateness, the cause of the world's difficulties, stems from the obsession with individual property and individual salvation; and it leads inevitably to the exploitation of the many by the few.

But Mary is troubled by the lack of love in Marxism and the Party; she turns to Cariss, the psychologist, in search of it. When she also fails to find love through Freud, she is ready to give up everything. But at this low point Markand appears to free her of Cariss and to re-establish her connection with Communism. Assuring her of the reality of love, he urges her to find growth and salvation in social action. She asks Lida, who is also an organizer, to live with her and to teach her devotion to the cause.

This theme of lack of love in Communism is, nevertheless, the point of "Si," the last note before a new octave. Mary and Lida organize a school for the children of the workers, but the party demands that it become a propaganda device and closes it until the two teachers can be satisfactorily indoctrinated. Then Lida and Kurt Doll fall in love, and the party seizes this natural event for propaganda purposes. The newlyweds will be sent as organizers to a textile strike, where they are sure to be killed by strikebreakers; but their violent deaths will make effective propaganda, especially in the bourgeois press, for "the respectable papers will make a fuss about the lynching of a respectable married couple." When romantic Mary protests the plan to party functionaries, they scornfully tell her to renounce feeling for blind obedience to directives. Shaken by the paradox of Communism, Mary says angrily, " 'They work day and night for the love of man, and they do not love.' " Then she is reminded of the analogous contradiction in the fundamentalist doctrines of her childhood, which were also dedicated to the salvation of mankind while denying love.

Desperately, Mary appeals to Markand to save Lida; but he refuses, having discovered in his own solitary search for truth that one grows strong by knowing that destruction is the ultimate fate of everyone. He takes Mary to an Irish bar at which the ragged drunks dance to an old hymn telling of the virgins who took their lamps and went to meet the Bridegroom. Each figure voices an idea or attitude—prophetic, esthetic, fundamentalist, Communistic—while crashing blindly into one another. This apocalyptic scene effectively challenges the validity or usefulness of any philosophy not centered in Wholeness, in the Person, and in love of life. Markand, however, is afraid. " 'My life is in a world I have not been simple enough to make pure,' " he tells her. " 'Not loving enough, perhaps, to keep from cruelty.' " But his words have brought Mary to wakefulness and to her solution for her problem:

> Mary knew that to wake was to love. To wake and to love were one.
> "There is a truth you don't know," she said to David Markand.
> "Yes."
> "You know only the truth to be feared . . . like God the Father."
> "Yes."
> "That Truth has a Son . . . not to be feared. It opens one's eyes . . . so gently, David."
> She got up, and he.
> In her loins the world stirred, sweet with her blood . . . huge.
> In his eyes, seeing this young woman, was an Answer, infinite, yet shaped by miracle for his hands and his mouth. The day was at the window of the room. They felt it there, the dawn gray and cold . . . standing together.

Thus the novel closes on the high note—"Si"—leading to the next octave, unlike the inconclusive note of Markand's story. While he was writing *The Bridegroom Cometh*, Frank sketched in Notebook XII a plan for a concluding volume, which throws some light on his conception of these two novels: ". . . . In Markand now mature as man, & Mary, mature as loving woman, the universe becomes fully dimensioned, by the consciousness—–intellectual, emotional, volitional, and above all *active*—–of man & woman. This is your triptych Saga: the Poem of the emergence of Communist Society in full human experience . . . . the crown of intellectual consciousness, and of conscious action (integrating the instinctive-intuitive-emotional-sensible-intellectual element of both the man & the woman)."

The union of David Markand and Mary Donald was destined to have no issue, however. The emergence of a Communist state became a nightmare instead of a poem, and Frank's personal world again fell apart. His marriage to Alma Magoon was breaking up; his hard work for Spain and for Marxist social reform had been unproductive. David and Mary could have no place in the terrible world coming into being: Armageddon, not the Bridegroom, was at hand.

CHAPTER *8*

The War Years

IN MAY AND JUNE of 1939 Frank made a third trip to Mexico, this time as a guest of the government. He toured the southern provinces with President Cárdenas and tried to interest the President in a plan for a continental magazine. His customary period of non-productivity after a major work was extended by his fretting over Hitler. He wrote an article on Cárdenas for *Foreign Affairs* and worked half-heartedly on a play; but, as the war tension grew, he sailed for England to visit his children. When World War II came, he brought his family back to New York and in November started sketching a book which explained America's relation to the crisis in Europe. He wrote *Chart for Rough Water: Our Role in a New World* in three months, and the book was published in April, 1940.

I *Chart for Action*

Although this short book was meant to be a call to arms, it is not just propaganda but, like all of Frank's writings, an expression of his organic philosophy, a characteristic which perhaps explains the remarkable prescience of his argument. As Bittner observes, "*Chart for Rough Water* shows so keen a perception of the dangers inherent, not only in American Isolationism, but in certain brands of Intervention, that it would be easy to forget that it was written in 1940 and to consider it analysis after the fact rather than prognostication."[1]

Essentially a simplified, direct application to a world threatened by Fascism of Frank's ideas already expounded in *The Re-discovery of America, Chart for Rough Water* is a kind of revolutionist's handbook; at the same time it is a brief, terse summation of his concept of the Person. Frank sees the war, like the Spanish civil struggle, as part of a general revolution against the old order of Western culture which has lost in its Fascist expression its initial concern with human values. Therefore, American isolationism is a fantasy, a projection of American idealism, which believes in and acts on the American's *idea* of himself rather than of reality, "even when the reality progressively and tragically refutes the idea."[2] Since America shares with Europe the psycho-cultural and the economic causes of the war, America cannot stay out of the conflict. The world crisis also lives within America, and the challenge is to rebirth or to catastrophe.

The history of the rise of the present conflict is to be found in "The Humiliation of Europe" since the Thirty Years' War, a humiliation attributable to a shift in values—to a shift, for example, from the medieval concern for salvation to the modern obsession with temporal well-being as a value. The individual ego, nurtured by man's awareness of the divine within him—an awareness which Frank identifies as "The Great Tradition" in Western society—now assumes self-sufficiency and dispenses with God or Cosmos. This projection of the ego—its rationale is capitalism—brings about the fall of Europe.

Frank now sees Communism as merely one of "The Desperate Remedies," which a modern arrogant Europe tries in place of "The Great Tradition." Communism fails to become more than a disguise for Russian Nationalism because it codifies Marx's rejection of the essence of religion, "the concept of the autonomous soul." But with Fascism, "for the first time, the humiliation of man becomes an open, aggressive doctrine." Frank next traces three forms that Fascism has known since 1922: the "larval," or gangster, stages of Mussolini; the rationalization of race infantilism with Hitler, "*the perfect antiperson*"; and the consummation of the two formative states in *fascized man*, "who believes he should rule the world because he is harder and more brutal than his elders." Greater than this threat from abroad, however, is the danger within, which Frank labels "The Inward 'Barbarian Invasion.'" These desperate political forms are dormant in America but are capable of developing into a native brand of Fascism.

To account for this paradoxical condition and at the same time to create a context for his solution for the problem, Frank traces the history of Western civilization in terms of the conflict between the individual and the Person. His synoptic version of this conflict becomes the simplest, clearest exposition of his philosophy in any of his writings. "Western civilization begins with the birth of the individual." Man acquires identity apart from that of group consciousness, and the integrity of his separate soul becomes the one true value. But he also develops an isolated, egocentric will which, free of the medieval synthesis, turns to reason and the machine instead of to God; and this act leads ultimately to the "humiliation" of European man,

> . . . not because the machine is evil, not because the individual is absolutely false, not because reason and a life of reason are wrong: *but because, as they have expressed themselves, the individual and reason and the machine represent a halfway house in the growth of man, a transition world from which man is challenged by his own growth to emerge in order to live more consciously in the depths of his whole nature; and from which at the same time he is pulled back and down, being still left with too many cultural tools and concepts of his unconscious past.*

By means of his egolatry Western man has achieved his adolescent stage, but this achievement has also created a period of crisis in which man must decide whether to mature to manhood or remain a child, a creature of infantile appetites. "Fascism is a symptom of the hunger to retreat in this crisis of man's adolescence——if need be to destroy his body and awakening soul, rather than struggle forward." The true maturing will be an act of spirit, the integrating of man's cultural history with a new spiritual awareness–the creation of the Person, who is "the individual integrated in his Cosmos . . . . the individual *through whom the Cosmos* speaks." But this "speaking" will involve action: "the soul becomes coincident with behavior and existence. Therefore it cannot be divided from its content, one aspect of which is social; nor can its deeds be divided from their content, one aspect of which is their social results."

Frank's concept of the Person is, therefore, at once dynamic and revolutionary: "A society where, not the individual, but *the potential person* is the norm of value, is one in which all intelligence is dedicated intrinsically——one might almost say 'selfishly'——to the public welfare. For the act of social justice is in the heart of the potential person who knows himself *a* heart of all men and of the universe; and whose knowing——however stumbling and full of error——is action."

Frank sees World War II as America's opportunity to develop its potential by preserving The Great Tradition. The war is but a symptom of a revolution, "a plenary readjustment to the new conditions of social life at a crisis in which the old order can no longer resist, or compromise with, those new conditions." America is a part of this revolution regardless of what it does about the war; the important thing is to realize that "To Be Creative, Revolution Must Be Religion." The real problem is to integrate this Great Tradition with American life, to base the nation's actions on religious values but not on historical religion: "Instead of the atomic and unreal *individual*, the *person*. Instead of salvation transmuted to another world because we are helpless here, the salvation of living our lives *now* by the knowledge, will and experience of *persons*. Instead of grace blindly bestowed by myth, the grace of our creative intuition of the God in us, leading us, with reason to help, to create human relationships, cities, countrysides, nations, in which *persons* can live." This is Frank's methodology for revolution. Through it, Frank would direct and revitalize art, education, politics: "The individual is quantitative; the person is qualitative." Only through the achievement of the Person will the potential Fascist in the individual be thwarted. Frank offers "*a principle of direction*" which will make revolution creative.

II *Summer Interlude*

Frank's intense concern with Fascism and the war stirred him to resign from the staff of the *New Republic* as a protest against its policy of neutralism. Almost as a kind of therapy he began to plan new books. One was to be the novel about the New York that his father knew, which Frank had first contemplated in 1931, when he was thinking about *The Death and Birth of David Markand.* The second was to be a philosophical treatise on the Person. Both books would require much preparatory work and were to draw Frank away from political activity with the exception of his propaganda tour of South America in 1942.

Unable to make an immediate start on the New York story, however, Frank became intrigued by what he calls in his notebook the "Theme of Dagny," an idea for a romantic narrative derived largely from his personal experience with a young graduate student but infused with his emotional reaction to Hitler's invasion of the Low Countries. In Notebook XIV he wrote: "I am recovering from a reeling, temporary derangement whose immediate cause was indubitably the blitzkrieg in Holland, Belgium, France." He then analyzed ways in which his personal life was influenced by these shocking developments; the novel was to reflect his version of the impact.

Early in June he began writing the tale, and it developed rapidly and easily, so that by September 25, he had completed a first draft. The revised manuscript was ready for Doubleday by the end of the year; but the publisher rejected the novel. Frank then shifted to Duell, Sloan and Pearce, who published *Summer Never Ends* on August 21, 1941.

Although subtitled *A Modern Love Story*, the novel is constructed around the "June and December" theme. Mortimer Crane, a middle-aged, successful corporation lawyer, falls in love with Dagny Petersen, a student who is just a little older than his son and daughter. Dagny appeals to him first as a contrast to his children, who seem bent upon self-destruction; but he soon begins to pursue her with all of the desperation of fatuous old lovers. Nevertheless, he continues to feel guilty about his children; and he makes a pretense of forcing them to save themselves by putting them out of his home—well supplied with cash!

Dagny is of course flattered by the attentions of a man of Mortimer's position and money, especially since the men in her life offer such depressing contrasts. Her father, Oskar, is an indolent, self-important, German-American Bundist; her brother, a colorless replica of his father. Her fiancé, Herbert Stein, is an unemployed Jewish lawyer, who is supported by a resentful sister. Dagny's mother, who works in a delicatessen, is the only strong-willed person around Dagny; and the two women dominate the weak, inferior men. Crane is a totally new experience for the girl, and she is easily attracted by his strength and aggressive love-making; but she tries to fight the attraction because she feels maternal toward the pathetic Herbert and is held by his dependence on her.

Crane tries to recapture his old idealistic, radical spirit—he had first achieved prominence as a labor lawyer—but only succeeds in annoying his conservative clients. Another symbolically destructive act is his foolish settlement of too much money on his wife, who is divorcing him; and his general confusion is revealed in his objecting to her plans to marry a man much older than she. Meanwhile, his life is filled with Dagny; and, when she momentarily responds to his ardor, he takes her: "he joyless, she utterly mute and dead."[3]

Baffled by the girl's passivity and subsequent rejection of him, Mortimer visits Judith Swift, his boyhood sweetheart whom he had left because he had been afraid that she would impede his drive for money and prestige. This interlude gives Frank an opportunity to inject his philosophy into this rather unphilosophical tale. Judith accuses Mortimer of irresponsibility in sacrificing their love for material goals; and she warns that there is only evil in Dagny, who feeds on the confusion of Mortimer and Herbert: "She doesn't know what evil is, I suppose, any more than you: being a modern girl. I know modern people don't believe in sin. . . . Your Dagny doesn't know yet. Because the world doesn't believe in evil. . . . *Evil can be innocent!*"

The only hope of countering man's talent for evil, she insists, is to be found in love "because nothing else works, nothing else wins! . . . Without love, or where it's weak, there's injustice, irresponsibility; there's strife and death—" Without love, evil lives off of the resulting bewilderment and separation of people: thus, business men, lawyers, and politicians "live off the confusions of the people." Judith has made her world live through love, although she would have preferred another one; Mortimer, on the other hand, has shaped his life by his desires, and he now has no stronghold of love.

The social manifestations of Judith's concept of evil are also revealed to Mortimer at a Washington golf club, where he meets the attaché of the Nazi Embassy. When Crane resolves to confront evil with love instead of fear, thereby supposedly routing the Nazi and winning Dagny, Frank is apparently trying to warn himself and perhaps America against such a soft doctrine of action in a time of crisis. At any rate, Mortimer's theory does not work for him; and no one has yet contended that love would have reformed Adolph Hitler. Mortimer offers Herbert a job in his office, but he is then goaded by the young man's hostility into citing his sexual relations with Dagny as proof of her love for him. When Herbert tells Oskar that Dagny has been having an affair with a Jew, the wronged father takes a gun from the Bund arsenal and goes to Crane's office to shoot him.

Mortimer, who is more intrigued than alarmed by the enraged parent, easily dissuades the bumbling Oskar by telling him that Herbert is really the only Jew involved. Crane then debases himself by bribing Oskar to press his case with Dagny while he uses Herbert's part in the episode to destroy him. He persuades Dagny to come to his apartment, but there she humiliates Mortimer and ends their affair by submitting to intercourse without any show of feeling. Meanwhile, Herbert, deeply ashamed of his use of Nazism against a rival yet still unable "to accept his shame and let it bleed away in living," plunges from Brooklyn Bridge murmuring, "There is God."

Crane, like David Markand, has discovererd that he must destroy his egocentric will before he can achieve rebirth: "He had acted by the law of what his life had been: here was the true humiliation:——the business man's law *to get what he could.* . . . Whatever Christ his fellows mouthed, *this* was the religion of their deeds day by day; and he had served them and they had paid him, because it was his religion also." Aware at last that there has been no place in his will for selfless love, Crane puts Oskar's revolver to his temple; but then a vision of his mother reveals the secret of true love—"it was God, and he knew it"—and he rushes back to his children to offer them the love that he has been insanely squandering upon Dagny.

Unfortunately, Mortimer Crane's rebirth does not redeem this sordid little tale of modern love; nor does Bittner's reading of the novel on multiple levels of meaning: "the Petersens are the idea we call Nazism—Oskar Petersen obviously the Nazi, stupid and brutal, authoritarian man; . . . Dagny an incipient Nazism in America. . . . Herbert is the Frank philosophy confronted with force, and lacking a method for handling force. . . . Mortimer's danger is alienation. He is strong enough, capable enough of transforming idea into action, but his action may go off in the wrong direction, independent of the things it ought to be a part of. On the level on which Oskar Petersen is the Nazi, Herbert is the Jew, and Mortimer is the well-meaning American."[4] The drawback to this ingenious reading is simply that the narrative does not support it. If Frank intends any such enriching analogy, his technique keeps him from achieving it.

The flatness of the characters and the sketchy development of situations suggest instead that Frank was preoccupied with his emotional problem of trying to live apart from his wife and children while still susceptible to romantic involvements. Nazism is merely an ironic adjunct to the familiar story of the infatuation of age with youth, and the David Markand theme of rebirth is dragged into the narrative to give some dignity and point to the trite situation. Mortimer Crane's discovery of the power of love is as unconvincing as any other rationalization of idiocy by a middle-aged swain. The resolution is a logical, legitimate application of Frank's organic philosophy, but the story is too frail to support it. *Summer Never Ends*, a failure on any count, is especially so in comparison with the two symphonic novels and their integration of the emotional and spiritual. Its failure is also one of form, for in it Frank slips back into the lyric mode without the poetry to sustain it. The result is that the novel is an exorcising of "the theme of Dagny" rather than a developing of it.

III *Mission in South America*

By the time *Summer Never Ends* was published, Frank was well into the writing of the story of New York, but he was not yet working easily or confidently. In April, in order to concentrate on the book, he turned down an offer of four thousand dollars by the Department of State for a lecture tour in South America designed to combat the widespread Fascist propaganda there; but he continued to be troubled by his refusal as letters from his friends in South America became more urgent. Pearl Harbor quickly resolved his indecision, and from mid-April until October, 1942, he lectured as an unofficial representative of the United States government in an effort to counter or weaken Fascist propaganda. His reputation and his reception in South American countries stirred active opposition. On August 1, he was declared *persona non grata* by Argentina, and the next day he was attacked by five toughs in his apartment in Buenos Aires. By making a great racket, he managed to frighten them away but not until they had cracked his head seriously enough to put him in a hospital and on the front page of the New York *Times*.

The publicity increased the effectiveness of his tour, but it also intensified the efforts of the Fascists to discredit him. Leaflets slandering him were distributed wherever he was scheduled to speak, and pro-Axis newspapers attacked him viciously; but he was too popular in South America to be harmed by such criticism and moved triumphantly through the land as a symbol of the anti-Fascist cause. In addition to Argentina, he lectured in Brazil, Chile, Uruguay, Peru, and Colombia; these lectures were collected and published in Buenos Aires under the title *Ustedes y Nosotros*. Upon his return to New York in October, Frank was given a testimonial dinner by the Union for Democratic America in recognition of his services. The attack on him by the thugs, followed by a series of articles that he wrote for *Collier's* magazine, gave him more publicity than usual; and he tried to exploit it by turning his journal record of his tour into a book—*South American Journey* (1943).

The book is not as topical or dated as its origins suggest, and

Frank is never dull as a commentator on cultural history. Furthermore, the book is not just a travelogue or a journal. Frank's tour merely provides the framework for his comments on the history, art, politics, and people of the countries visited. His impressions of the "face" and the "body" of Brazil, which are especially searching and vivid, are representative. Frank sees Brazil like the United States in many ways but without the America's blighting race-consciousness. Brazil's assimilation of mixed races and her freedom from hereditary castes signify a kind of elemental democracy of tremendous potential which will eventually outgrow the need for dictators like Vargas, who is "the product of a politically and economically backward country which has given up none of its ideals of democracy."[5]

The book is not limited to cultural history, however; it includes the record of Frank's battles with the Fascists, a tale of violence and skulduggery which sometimes reads like the scenario of a spy picture. In these sections the emphasis is upon people: the politicians and the professors, the journalists and the artists, the dictators and the diplomats that Frank encountered. In catching the essence of the personalities of these friends and enemies, he reveals a richness of perception characteristic of his cultural views but often absent from his drawing of characters for his novels. The sketches of politicos like Vargas, Castillo, Aranha, Ortíz, and Justo, for example, are especially enlightening and should be useful even today to a student of South American politics.

Although *South American Journey* in form has the loose, episodic pattern of its source, the underlying theme is Frank's concept of organic wholeness. Behind his concern with the immediate war is his preoccupation with what he calls "The Deep War"—the conflict between an over-rationalized, super-mechanized, materialistic mode of living and the intuitive, religious, spiritual way implicit in the hope for a New World. This hope and this promise are threatened by the egocentric will to power of totalitarian states, but the danger is not limited to them. It exists wherever and whenever a perverted power drive reduces humanity to slavery, whether it be by the State, the Machine, or the Race. Furthermore, this deeper war will continue after the Axis powers have been crushed, for it is located within the self and its battle can only be won through the organic development of the Person.

In fighting this inner battle, Frank suggests, as he did in his other books on America Hispana, that the Yankee turn to his Latin neighbors for inspiration and guidance. "The peoples of America Hispana, politically and economically our backward disciples, have played the leading role in the deepening of the democratic concept. This they have done not by overt doctrine, but by their racially, aesthetically and intellectually more free and more organic ways of living." Herein is the basis for the need for greater understanding and cooperation between the Americas.

In effect, Frank insists there are three Americas, Brazil being as distinct from America Hispana as from the United States and Canada. These three Americas desperately need one another if they are to achieve their individual potentials; they should become One America, with an island psychology instead of a continental one: "The American hemisphere must become an island dedicated to the democratic will of creating persons; implemented by the technics that alone can give to man the peace, leisure and knowledge to become a person." In his analysis of these Americas, Frank writes a clear, concise statement of his theory of the Person which is, in effect, a summary of all of his earlier partial characterizations and a definite linking of the personal and the social wills:

> The person is not the mere individual. He is the individual aware of his organic and purposive part in the social group and in the Cosmos. These two integrations are not divisible in life; only the needs of analysis may separate them. Integration in the group (which includes concentric bodies from family and work-union to sovereign state and federated inter-nation) requires social justice, race freedom, an ethic of mutual respect and service. Integration in the Cosmos implies the experiences and activities of the arts and religion. And of course, these activities cannot be dissolved from the individual's social and public conduct. Both integrations enlist all man's centers: his instinctive and emotional life, his will, his aesthetic and intellectual thinking. Only when the individual functions on all these planes and toward all these directions, is he a person. And democracy is the one principle of life which requires this wholeness of behavior; which therefore ineluctably moves toward the development of persons. . . . In the materialistic forms of socialism and communism that make an absolute of human society, the individual's direct conduit and relation to the Cosmos atrophies and disappears.
>
> Democracy, in the complete sense . . . must include not only all men, but *the whole man.* Freedom must mean growth not only for all men, but for every phase and dimension of the man.

The United States should make itself qualified and ready to provide the kind of leadership which will enable the three Americas to effect a union based upon the freedom "that dwells in justice and . . . the knowledge that is love."

IV *The Jews*

While *South American Journey* was being printed, Frank made a coast-to-coast lecture tour and then returned to New York and his draft of the new novel. But while he was trying to start it again, he wrote reviews and articles and then discovered, while checking through his list of publications, that he had written in various articles what was in reality a kind of series on Jewish problems. Since he had long been contemplating writing a book about the Jews, he decided to organize these essays into a collection while he was in Reno waiting for a divorce from Alma. From Reno he went to San Francisco, where he married Jean Klempner, who had been his secretary during the writing of *South American Journey*. In October, after another lecture tour in the West, Frank moved back to New York and resumed work on the collection which was finished early in 1944 and published in August.

The Jew in Our Day is not the book that Frank intended to write about Jews; it is merely an anthology of eight articles which first appeared in such widely disparate publications as the *Saturday Evening Post* (1942), *Menorah Journal* (1926), *The Synagogue* (1941), *Contemporary Jewish Record* (1943). In a long Introduction, Reinhold Niebuhr raises questions about Frank's views that the author attempts to answer in a postscript.

Despite Hitler and the increase in anti-Semitism in the United States, Frank insists in these articles that the Jews' basic problem is religious rather than racial, ethnic, or political. Jews are persecuted simply because they are different; but they are different only in their attempt to live by a tradition which is characterized by "the seeking of a way of life which would bring down to earth, in terms of everyday behavior, the idea of a universal yet intimate God who was lovingly concerned with the life of every one of His children."[6] Thus, the Judaic tradition affirms knowledge also found in the Great Tradition of the Western world and the democratic projection of the latter in the United States: the knowledge "that life has meaning, and that every man, woman and nation can discover life's meaning—which is, to win the world, under God, through justice, mercy and love, for the brotherhood of man."

The Jews have survived because their values were made functional in the world. Their personal and social actions were expressions of wholeness, of an essential unity between vision and performance. Now, however, the Jews face a new crisis, one created by the challenge of the modern world to all traditional values. In their too-ready acceptance of the shallow, superficial materialism of the contemporary civilization, especially in the United States, the Jews betray their heritage and in doing so weaken not only themselves but also democracy. The roots of democracy are religious; only the *whole* man can be free. But the whole cannot be nurtured on acquisitiveness and material comforts. Only by rejecting a godless way of life and by re-discovering the traditional values can the Jews help to cure the world of its sickness, a sickness which also finds one natural expression in anti-Semitism. If the Jews work for the things in life which nourish the whole person and for social justice, their "separateness will be again their bond with all the world."

The Jew in Our Day, a mere collection of essays, was not a satisfactory book, either artistically or commercially; but it did help Frank to return to productive work on the novel. He retired with his new wife to his studio at Truro, Massachusetts, and completed a draft of *Island in the Atlantic* in about twelve months; and it was published in September, 1946, almost six years after he started writing it.

CHAPTER *9*

Cosmic Knowledge

NOTEBOOK XV reveals that when Frank had started writing *Island in the Atlantic* in 1941, he saw in his father's story a chance to defend the Jew in America: "my novel in its *deep* revelation of the espousal of American life—deeply—by the Jew will, if it is read, be a great reply to the poison implicit in the thought of 'Yankees & Cavaliers' like Beard, Nock, et al . . . the implication that the Jews are (however 'admirable') outsiders to American life, with at best a mechanical—not chemical—relation to the Gentile. Jonathan Hartt is a Jew who never doubts or misprises his Jewishness: yet at the book's close, he will be revealed as an American hero."

Island in the Atlantic, however, is more than a fictionized story of Julius Frank or a defense of Jewishness. It is instead the story of Jonathan Hartt's quest for a kind of knowledge which will provide a valid rationale for faith, hope, and love. "Both the Christian and the Rational Empirical 'knowledge' are obsolescent," Frank contends in the notebook entry. "The basal, the tragic-crucial task of our time is to lay the foundations of a cogent knowledge, within which man may again have faith—whence hope—whence (the greatest of these—the true food) Love." This cogent knowledge is, of course, an intuitive sense of the Whole, of organic unity.

I *Manhattan Island*

Island in the Atlantic tells the story of three generations during the crucial period of change in the United States between the Civil War and World War I. Its structure is symphonic, like that of *The Death and Birth of David Markand* and *The Bridegroom Cometh*; yet despite the greater number of characters and episodes in it—the action, for example, is not confined to New York but moves to Ohio and eventually Paris—the narrative is more tightly constructed than in the other symphonic novels and more effectively integrates the protagonists and their milieu.

Frank's handling of point of view and of time contribute to this structural unity. Always an experimenter with the treatment of time in his narratives, Frank in this novel discards the "linear" presentation for the symbolic. In keeping with the Mayan rubric used as a motto for the book—"In the eye of the Eternal, each man's life is a day"—Frank compresses the sprawl of over half a century into one day and divides the story into two parts: "Morning," which reveals Jonathan Hartt entrapped by the "old" knowledge associated with his life in New York; and "Afternoon," which shows Jonathan slowly developing into the Person. Within these two divisions, each part is centered on a crucial day in the life of Jonathan or of the nation; and most of the events are recounted through Jonathan's consciousness. Form therefore becomes theme, and the conventional sprawl of the historical panoramic novel is eliminated.

The first "day" is July 13, 1863, a date which is established by events, since Frank mentions no specific dates in the narrative. This section of the novel is entitled "Hope" to identify the emotion felt by immigrants to the city of New York and by young Jonathan. But on this day the irony of that hope is depicted in the riots against the draft for the Civil War in which drunken Irish "patriots" hang Negroes and fire the homes of the wealthy. Fifteen-year-old Jonathan, hearing his parents dismiss the rioting, reflects critically: "Mother, noblest of women, did not know everything. Even in Jefferson's America, democracy was not yet perfect: look at Tammany and the Rebels. Even in free America, even with the slaves all free, there might still remain *some* unfinished business from the American and French Revolutions."[1]

The schemes of the cynical leaders in the city, like Grosvenor Cleeve, to exploit the social unrest politically and financially deepens the ironic contrast between the hope and the reality. In a secret meeting, these leaders decide to reject the offer of Connecticut troops for reinforcements so that the mobs, composed wholly of Democrats, will have more time to create by their behavior hostility for their party. With luck, it is pointed out, the rioters may even attack Greeley's *Tribune* and also burn out the dreadful slums: "The Metropolitans . . . can protect the large buildings; the new Guard of businessmen can hold *our* houses——."

Grosvenor Cleeve represents the robber baron of the 1860's, determined to retain power until money is firmly in control of the city and eventually of the nation. His power complex has already lost him the love of his wife and earned the hatred of his only son, Evan. The parents now carry on a silent, bitter struggle for the soul of their son. During one of the riots, Evan meets Jonathan and establishes a relationship which affords the major contrasts and tensions in the novel while at the same time picturing typical upper- and middle-class attitudes during the period.

The riots presage the death of the various "hopes" developed in this section and the stormy death of the old forms of knowledge represented by the Judeo-Christian and rationalist traditions. Yet hope persists in all of the characters except Emma Cleeve in books I and II, although the subtitle "Mirages" for the second indicates the nature of the optimism. Book II is composed of three widely separated days during which hope proves to be a mirage. The first day is in 1871, when Emma Cleeve, having lost all hope for the potential victory of love in her relations with her husband and her son, commits suicide. On that same day Jonathan Hartt and Evan Cleeve become law partners, a hopeful projection of sentimentality over reason and instinct.

The next pivotal day is in 1877, when Jonathan and Greta Mendis agree to marry; but it is already apparent that Jonathan will stifle a vital spark in her personality in trying to make her conform to his righteousness. This day has a brief prelude in July 4, 1876, when the gentle, bumbling, ever-optimistic father of Jonathan, Joseph Hartt, dies while in the background the Centennial Exposition in Philadelphia ignores the promise of America expressed in a song for the occasion composed by an old gray poet who "had hobbled on foot a good part of the way from his home in Camden." The third day is in 1889, when Jonathan, still rigidly righteous, refuses to compromise his principles in order to save Evan, whose crooked deals with Tammany politicians must be exposed. But with the end of his relationship with Evan and the subsequent deterioration of his marriage with Greta, Jonathan's period of hope comes to a close, although he tries to transfer his dreams to his son, Jefferson.

Book III, entitled "The Waters Flow Through the Land" to suggest Evan's aimless wandering to the mainland of the Midwest, is a kind of interlude in which Evan's life apart from the "island" of New York is pictured in counterpart to the childhood and adolescence of Jefferson Hartt. Evan finds a shaky anchorage in

Elysium, a river town easily recognizable as Cincinnati, Ohio. There he plays violin in the symphony, lives in a boarding house run by a colorful family of Bohemian eccentrics, and marries Rachel Lorne, a gentle, naïve, Quaker schoolteacher. But in his drive toward self-destruction, Evan deliberately fails at his work and in his marriage; and he encourages his daughter, Rebecca, to hate him as he has supposedly hated his father. Evan is another version of the satanic personality found in most of Frank's novels, the bright, clever servants of evil who tempt and challenge the good man while trying to destroy him.

As Evan slips toward the gutter, Jonathan struggles against the corruption of the Gilded Age. He is sustained by his memory of the hope enshrined in the city of his youth and by the hope now centered in his son. But he realizes that he will need to find a new kind of knowledge to develop the potential of Jefferson: "Nothing in his well-planned life had come out as he hoped; not his career of public service, not his friendship and partnership with Evan, not his marriage. Something somewhere along the years had gone wrong. He remembered the last silent word of his father: what had it been but hope? His father had never known him; his father had had faith, his mother had had will; the two, faith and will, were not enough, were no substitute for knowledge. . . ." For Evan, the hope of "Morning" ends with his death from pneumonia on Jonathan's fiftieth birthday: "Evan had been a violent man because the one unity he could reach was death."

Book IV in Part Two, "Afternoon," is entitled "Bread Upon the Waters" to mark the entrance of the third generation with its burden of inherited hope. Jonathan has a sordid affair with a mercenary client because he feels the need, in his consciousness of the death of his hopes, to revolt against his constricted life and to learn somehow to love. As he climbs the stair to Louella Lake's apartment, the scene shifts to Evan's daughter, Rebecca, who is incapable of loving anyone because she is enslaved by her almost demonic belief in rationalism. A fashion designer, she starts for New York; enroute she meets Jefferson, who is returning from Paris, where he has been studying architecture. His subsequent affair with Rebecca is in counterpoint to Jonathan's with Mrs. Lake.

Unable to love Jefferson, Rebecca is nevertheless attracted to a violent, egocentric anarchist, Marius Schmitt, the son of one of the Hartts' maids during Jonathan's childhood. Jonathan's clever, unscrupulous brother, Reuben, has swindled the Schmitts of the little farm which had been their one "hope"; and warped, bitter Marius is one consequence of that sharp dealing. But it requires the skill of the pragmatic Reuben to extricate Jonathan from Mrs. Lake's attempt at blackmail. When Rebecca flees to Paris, Marius and Jefferson follow her, while Jonathan tags along to watch over his son. Jefferson, having confessed his adulterous relationship with Rebecca, is supposedly going at his wife's insistence to find out exactly what Rebecca means to him.

The last book of "Afternoon" reveals that the "bread cast upon the waters" returns "Knowledge." Marius, Rebecca, and Jefferson settle in a little cottage on an island off the coast of Oléron. When Marius and Jeff fight, Marius is killed; and Jonathan is mystically summoned by a vision to the island. Jeff is released by the police on a charge of involuntary manslaughter; and the episode also frees him of Rebecca, who is now fully revealed as a lost soul bent upon destruction. Enroute to America on the newly commissioned steamer *Cosmopolis*, Jeff asks his father if he believes in God; and Jonathan expresses the religious theme of the novel in his reply: "I don't believe in belief. . . . Knowledge is what is needed, Jeff. Not belief. Belief goes wrong!" When the liner strikes an iceberg and starts to sink, Jonathan acts upon his hard-won knowledge, pushes his son into a lifeboat, and goes down with the ship.

The import of Jonathan's action has already been established before the disaster in his change in attitude during the closing scenes of the narrative. On the promenade deck he has looked at the doomed men and women and reflected bitterly that at such moments each is alone, untouched by anything—the stars, the sea, or one another:

> Jonathan's heart broke because he could not love them; he too was alone. If they touched him—they who were his world and generation, it was to contempt. A mean world it had been, building a continent, spanning the seas, without love, without light. And he had fought it meanly: loveless and lightless men, the reformers, and he had been no better. Who had been better? Not the leaders. Only they who were so alien to their generation they could not even fight it. The desperate ones! Evan . . . not Evan's sleek, successful father. Marius and Jeff who had killed him . . . not Jeff's father. There was hate in his heart.—I cannot bear to hate them, I cannot bear to hate myself!

So he pushes Jeff overboard near a lifeboat. He then crawls back to the promenade deck, where the band is playing a hymn, and reflects: "Now they knew; now they were together. And he was with them at last, where he belonged. Jeff lived, and he could love them. Each of them was like his son who was a coward, as was he, as were they. Jeff in passive violence had killed; so had he, so had they. Each of them was doomed and in the saving of one whom they loved, was saved. He loved his son; now that he had saved him, he was free: free to love them who were all sons of guilt together; free to love himself." Thus, Jonathan becomes the Person, aware at last of himself and of his organic relationship with the Whole, possessed finally of the knowledge of the ultimate unity of man, men, and cosmos—a knowledge which passeth understanding but makes one free.

Like the other symphonic novels, however, *Island in the Atlantic* is too open-ended to give a compelling sense of the reality of Wholeness. Jonathan is a symbol of a dying century; Jeff, the hope of the new one. Yet there is little evidence in the novel that Jeff will prove equal to that hope, that he will even develop beyond his escape from the kind of bondage represented by Rebecca. Therefore, Jonathan's achievement of awareness may have little or no significance for the society of the new century. Frank has clearly discounted the potentialities of Jeffersonian liberalism and Marxist collectivism for social growth by showing that the faith of Joseph and Jonathan Hartt in the former has not been productive of good; nor has the collectivism of big business —which, ironically, relates it to Marxism—or the violence of radical Socialism brought salvation. New knowledge is needed, but Jonathan's kind of new knowledge seems little more than a wistful hope in the irrational world of the twentieth century.

This inadequacy in the social dimension of the novel should not, on the other hand, detract from Frank's success in creating the sense of an era. He makes these crucial years in the life of the nation live, and they live especially vividly in the opening sections having to do with a city and a century of hope. He achieves this effective picture of a nation at war with itself and of its potential by making his father's New York a sensory experience. To do so, he read omnivorously in the popular literature of the period, including the drama, trying to see, hear, even smell the city. New York emerges as an entity and as a symbol of the years from 1863-1912 while focusing the action of the narratives.

"Somehow, without losing the realism and sweep of the symphonic novel, *Island in the Atlantic* has in it the poetic quality of *City Block*."[2] This skillful blend of diverse yet colorful elements makes it the most interesting of these novels. Whether it is the "best" of the novels depends upon the reader's taste in form, since the early "lyric novels" cannot logically or fairly be compared to the symphonic narratives. In view of his success with the latter form in this novel, it is doubly regrettable that Frank did not choose to go on with the type and carry the Person into the present. His next novel, which was to be concerned with the age of the bomb, did not have the symphonic structure.

II *The Bomb*

Writing in Notebook XIX early in 1947, Frank had this to say of his books.

> In all these works, there was present——and this explains perhaps why they were seldom popularly received——the intention (a) to create organic aesthetic form; (b) to concretize, in modern terms, an experience, a methodology, or Religion; (c) to discover this Religion in our world and to apply it to the basic problems (from aesthetic to political) of our world. From now on to the end . . . this unitary-triune intention must possess me. . . . My projected novels, my Re-discovery of Man, will be the articulations . . . of this final phase of my creative will.

One projected articulation was *A Cottage at Land's End*, a poetic drama or novel about the atom bomb which was to dramatize "the violent World-Action of our time in deeply personal 'peace' terms."

After some false starts and considerable procrastination, Frank shaped the opening scenes. Determined to avoid the sprawl of the symphonic novel, he recorded in the notebook his plans for "an intense, sharply focused story: it should have the essence, but not the extension——the quality but not the quantity——of the World Scene." But this change in form created difficulties, and he welcomed an interruption by young labor leaders seeking his participation in a conference on political action. He wrote a preamble to the agenda for the conference, attended the meetings, gave the opening address at the American Congress of Art Teachers, and then settled at Truro to work on the novel. He completed a rough draft by mid-May, the revisions by October; the book was finally published in May, 1948, with the title *The Invaders*.

Troubled, like every thinking person after Hiroshima, by the terrible new threat to mankind, Frank tries in *The Invaders* to show the import of the bomb for the individual. In the life of each of the typical Americans in the narrative the bomb bursts internally, bringing destruction to anyone who lacks an inner soundness or who has not attained the unity of the Person. When a new kind of bomb—it kills without destroying property—is dropped upon New York, it leads quickly to a military dictatorship and to an enemy attack with conventional atomic bombs.

The radio brings news of the first bomb to a cottage on the New England coast which is occupied by Mark Terry, a retired architect; his second wife, Bianca; and their baby son, Christopher. The disaster literally reaches their refuge in the form of "invaders" from the city: Mara, Mark's first wife; Bayard and Beth, their adolescent children; and Lew Dachill, Mara's lover. Mara now hates Mark and resents his happiness with Bianca. The effect of her hatred on Bayard and Beth is an example of the internalizing of the *essence* of the atomic explosion. The childrens' feelings toward Mark are a confused mixture of natural love and nurtured hatred: Bayard sides with his mother; Beth is sympathetic toward Mark but deeply disturbed by the break between her parents.

These "invaders" are joined by one from nearby Boston, Clare Locke, a veteran who has had his face burned away during World War II by a bomb dropped from an Allied plane. Born a Jew, trained at Massachusetts Institute of Technology as a mathematician, Clare became a Communist and, disgusted with a society that bred war, requested combat in order to seek death. He had met Bianca at a dance and had corresponded with her until the injury to his face when he had suddenly stopped writing. Having scornfully rejected government aid, he has been living off his old father and bitterly expounding his new religion that man has no soul, that he is nothing more than an equation in biochemistry. Now Clare has sought out Bianca in his acceptance of the coming end of the world because her touch had suggested the reality of love in a world of illusion.

Mara becomes the threat to the idyllic little world of the Terry home that the bomb is to mankind. She brings hate and Bianca tries to throw her out; but Mark, idealistically searching for some creative attitude toward hatred in the world, rejects his wife's simple, instinctive reaction. "Why are we here?" he says quietly. "If a world is to be born, a world must go down and needs to be destroyed. . . . We must not exclude, we must transform! And the wonderful creative act must begin humbly——and everywhere!"[3]

Later, when Mara spews her bitterness over the household, Mark stubbornly insists upon the need for meeting hatred with love. He sees Mara as a by-product of a culture that spawns war, famine, moral breakdown, shallowness, and despair: "And how else could it be, with the atomic self the fetish and the Law . . . with technology, ideology and God the tools of the atomic self?" To throw Mara out, Mark reasons, would be to surrender to her world, the bomb's world. "This individual fight of his was man's fight for survival . . . . but only if humble men and women accepted their share in what was universal could a human world be born." He tries to explain to the sneering, abusive Mara, saying: "we few people in this house with a white fence around it must learn to help each other live, or there's no hope anywhere. . . ." And then, when Bianca tries to force Mara to leave, Mark says sadly, "People are hurt . . . and in self-defense hurt others. And these always in self-defense hurt others: the endless bloody circle! With all the inertia of tradition, right, duty and love, to keep it going and to keep us caught! Someone must jump out of it, Bianca!"

Beth is the first victim of the circle. She gives herself to Clare Locke, half in self-pity, to rebuke her parents for hurting her. Then, when Locke refuses to take her back to Boston with him, she swims too far out into the sea and drowns; but she might have been saved if Locke and Bayard had been watching her instead of arguing about her. Once again the separatist ego claims its victim. Now Beth's death brings the crisis for Mara whose reaction is meant to focus and illumine the themes of the book in the suggestive, incandescent manner of poetry.

As the radio announces the end of the state of siege in New York and the establishment of a military dictatorship in Washington, Mark carries his daughter's body into the cottage. Mara, insane from her sense of loss, need, and rage, smothers Bianca's baby Christopher in a convulsive embrace; and the circle claims its second victim. Bianca's shriek is heard in the cottage as a bum in Times Square hears the shriek of the city as a conventional atomic bomb releases its mushroom ring. It is by Mara's act that Frank hopes to make the substance of his novel incandescent and to articulate the respective essences of the characters. The deaths of Beth and of Christopher are the crux of the book, Frank notes in his journal, and must provide the light which will transform the whole episode: "if that light fails to materialize it remains an episode, and my book a failure. But preaching, moralizing, exposition of ideas do not furnish fuel for light, in a work of art—a Poem. The substance must be incandescent."

Although Bayard now wants to stay with his father, Mark sends him away with Mara because she has such a great need for him. Locke threatens to take Bianca with him to win her as she begins to hate her husband, but then Mark's pain makes Locke refuse Bianca's request to go with him. In the final confrontation of Mark and his wife, he begs her not to follow the old responses to disaster and run away; she must face her loss now and in so doing become transfigured. "Pain was the sole human power (Oh, this stricken generation boasting its feeble atomic might and neglecting man's true power!) . . . man's creative act with pain was his sole difference from animal and insect. And only if men were formed who lived by this, who grasped pain at its crisis . . . not running from it, not hiding from it, not turning it always against others . . . could Man inherit the earth."

Mark clings desperately to his belief as Bianca leaves. He has wrongly tried to impose his knowledge upon her who could know only as a mother knows. Yet "what he had done to them all must not have been in vain. There was Cause for what he had done; although fleshed in his fumbling and failure, there was Truth, and he must not betray it. . . ."

Frank's notebook reveals that he did not arrive at this ending easily but first had to discover the falsity of a happy resolution. "In real life, doubtless, they could live on together and he work out his 'payment,' living with her. But in the simple forms of my tragedy, this could not be indicated. . . . Mark must suffer & lose Bianca, in order to gain the sympathy of the reader, & give him his catharsis. . . ." But Mark's failure to break the circle of hate in time does not necessarily indicate that his theory is wrong. It may still prove to be right and productive. Bayard has been drawn to him and Bianca is pregnant; they may return to him because he has acted with love toward them. The nation, on the other hand, that blindly responds to force with force cannot win. It will either be destroyed from without by superior force or from within by the self-destroying elements released. The circle will not be broken.

The Invaders, a thesis novel, suffers from the inherent defects of the type. The major characters—Mark, Mara, Clare, Beth—do not carry gracefully or persuasively the "idea," which is no more extreme or impractical than the exhortation to turn the other cheek. But Frank has not succeeded in endowing Mark Terry with enough personality to make his vision of life viable. He is gentle but tactless, kind but righteous; he is given to the kind of eloquent sententiousness that can on occasion startle even himself: "Bianca had seen Mark stop; the terror of his words revealing the hated Hitler as hero fused in the silence. . . ." Mark comes too near fanaticism to evoke sympathy or to permit catharsis; he stirs only pity for his high-level bumbling, so that there is an embarrassing kind of ironic appropriateness in his metaphor: "Men are moles with a beginning of eyesight. In their blindness, they had all the senses they required for mole habits. Now, with their new dim sight those habits are traps! . . . They see too much to be moles, they don't see enough to be men. That's modern history in a nutshell! All our institutions, our ways of thinking and above all of feeling, are the sufficient habits of blind moles."

Mara, Clare, and Beth acquire only identity and not personality through their somewhat melodramatic roles; and, since they cannot create interest as people, their actions are not compelling or convincing. Of these three, Mara is the most effective, perhaps only because her kind of evil is usually more dramatic in a character than goodness. Like many novelists, Frank is more successful with his satanic characters than with his Christ figures; but Mara, however, does not achieve the stature of villainous Tom Rennard or Evan Cleeve; like Rebecca, she does not represent much more than bitchery. Locke is almost a robot, as mechanical and grotesque as his rebuilt face; Beth, for all her sensitivity to the hate in her mother, is the adolescent romantic given to gestures.

The artificiality of these major characters, the "created" quality about them, reduces them and their tale to the limitations of allegory which blunt the potential—and intented—impact of the narrative. In *The Invaders* Waldo Frank is more the social critic and philosopher than the novelist. Mark Terry's concept of living can be understood and even accepted, along with Jesus Christ's; but Mark Terry's story cannot because of the novelist's drift toward allegory, especially in his drawing of characters. *The Invaders* is a better novel than *Summer Never Ends*, but it should not even be compared with *Island in the Atlantic*. In view of the importance of its theme, one wishes that Frank's novel were equal to its subject.

CHAPTER 10

Old and New Worlds

EARLY IN 1948, waiting for page proof of *The Invaders*, Frank, in casting about for his next project, sketched the outline of a book frequently mentioned in his journals: a definitive analysis of his philosophy to be called *The Rediscovery of Man*. He also jotted down some ideas for short stories, a form virtually ignored by him since 1922. Before Frank could implement either of these projects, he was called to South America again: he accepted an invitation from Rómulo Gallegos to attend his inauguration as President of Venezuela, an event signifying the accession to political power of the generation of rebels who had read Frank in the late 1920's and been nourished by his vision of the Americas.

During the week of festivity, Frank discussed with his admirers in the new government the cultural needs of Venezuela. Rómulo Betancourt, the Provisional President of the junta which had overthrown the military dictatorship, suggested that Frank write an interpretation of Simon Bolivar and his significance for the modern age. The subject was too appealing and the financial arrangement too attractive for Frank to resist. He returned to cultural history, and for the next three years immersed himself in the world of Bolivar, visiting the scenes of his life and reading the mass of source material.

Before the end of 1948, the Gallegos government was overthrown; but the new government, not wanting to appear anticultural, honored Frank's contract. *The Birth of a World* was published in September, 1951, in the United States and England, to be followed by a French translation; but the Venezuelan government delayed issuance of a Spanish translation for several years.

I *Simon Bolivar*

The subtitle of the study, *Bolivar in Terms of his Peoples*, indicates Frank's characteristic organic approach to cultural history. He based his work on scholarship, but he wrote it for the general reader. For Bolivar is a product of "the peoples, the cities, the arts, the folklore and the *land*";[1] he personifies the struggle of his people to emerge from chaos into order and unity. He identifies many of the values of the Hispanic world, values whose timeliness relate his world to the Modern Age. Most significantly for Frank, Bolivar is a stirring symbol of the principle of wholeness because he "translated into act Spain's mystic will to make an empire . . . not for power like Rome, not for profit like Britain . . . *for all men and for the whole man.*" Thus it seems to Frank "that Bolivar, if we *experience* him, may signify today as much to the United States as to America Hispana. The meaning of this for the world, if it is true, given the strategic place and potential creative power of the United States, is manifest."

Bolivar's contemporary significance lies in the man himself, in his vision of the "Atlantic World" which Frank had first sketched in *America Hispana*—an Atlantic world which must eventually embrace Western Europe. Bolivar failed because "he relied too desperately on the State, and . . . equated the State with himself"; he released chaos and it doomed him. But in revolution there is creation: Bolivar's campaigns have vanished yet his dream of a new world is a living challenge for man to create one out of chaos, a challenge which becomes ever more urgent as the need grows tragically greater. "Bolivar's defeat lighted a sacrifice-fire by which we may behold America and begin to create it."

By projecting Bolivar's evolution into the Person—"In his life-work, not in the hour-by-hour texture of his years, he was an integrated person"—against a backdrop of the land and the people, Frank attempts the kind of symphonic structure used in the social novels. He organizes his voluminous material into three books: in "The Kingdoms," he sketches the cultural and political conditions in Spain's Northern colonies from the time of their founding and in counterpoint tells of the lineage and "Education of a Provincial Prince," which includes Bolivar's mystic rebirth after his first defeat, like the rebirth of the hero of one of Frank's novels or even of Frank himself. Book Two, "The Peoples," carries the action from the establishment of the river capital of Angostura, in July, 1817, through the major military campaigns, to Bolivar's departure from Lima, after his Constitution had been rejected, in September, 1826. Book Three, "The Man," traces the story of his return to Venezuela and thereafter his string of political defeats until his death on December 17, 1830.

It is a dramatic tale, and Frank fully exploits its dramatic qualities by treating the protagonists like characters in a play and by framing their relations in acts of the drama. Páez, Santander, Manuela Sáenz, San Martin are especially memorable among the horde of characters acting out this tragedy of blood. For the story of the Spanish conquest of America and the subsequent struggle of the enslaved for freedom are the bloodiest and most depressing spectacles in the sad record of man's inhumanity to man. And, as in any pure tragedy, even the hero, Bolivar, is flawed, being guilty of treachery and atrocity. Frank sees Bolivar's attempt to realize his vision by force as his tragic error, and the biographer does not stint the bloodletting. Yet Frank memorably catches the vision, as in the following passage—a good illustration of his skill in fusing style and theme:

> Bolivar was the last true king of the Hispanic spirit. To his great predecessors, freedom meant the grace of the Church, and all Spain's soldiers and inquisitors were there to force this freedom upon every man. Bolivar refused the theocratic definition within the Necessity of the Church, but he retained the concept of a vast political unit, of *its* necessity and of salvation within it. After Ayacucho, the huge Andean land from Venezuela to Chile seemed about to become a modulation of Spain's ideal empire: there would be no slaves, in terms of modern liberalism men would be free within a great but aloof state; in lieu of Spain's dissolving City of God, a City of Man which Bolivar's Panama would project to the hemisphere and beyond it. Of course, the canvas tore before the picture could be painted; and Bolivar knew. But while he knew, his fighting within the sense of history, his conscious destiny of failure, was regal. Only little kings succeed, he knew; the great who greatly strive become heroes of tragedy. He acted his tragic part.

II *The Spirit Within*

Upon completing *The Birth of a World*, Frank resumed work on the short stories which composed his last published work of fiction, *Not Heaven.* He had begun writing the stories—the themes having been recorded in a special notebook started during the early 1920's—during the spring of 1948 while he was waiting for a contract for the Bolivar book. Between April 22 and June 21, he completed rough drafts of eight of the tales and, somewhat to his amazement, discovered a potential unifying theme which became his justification for calling the collection a novel. The theme is recorded in Notebook XIX: "All on earth (as Mephisto states) is Hell 'that is not Heaven.'" At this point, however, the Bolivar study received the official sanction of the new revolutionary government of Venezuela; and Frank did not resume work on the story cycle until 1952. He completed it late in that year, and *Not Heaven* was published in May, 1953, by Hermitage House.

As in *City Block* Frank sees the story cycle in *Not Heaven* as a novel: "A Novel," according to the subtitle, "in the Form of Prelude, Variations, and Theme." But in *City Block* there is at least unity of place and in some instances, as when characters move through several stories, unity of action. Lacking even these simple connectives, *Not Heaven* requires a rather specialized concept of a novel, which Frank boldly provides in "An Aside to the Reader," placed *after* the last story. He cites precedents for ignoring classical assumptions about the novel—assumptions which stem from Graeco-Roman and Judeo-Christian culture with their traditional premises of time and character; thus, a story cycle may reveal a primitive or dynamic unity adequate for a novel. For example, *Not Heaven* "has, in place of unifying plot, a unifying theme which grows, as the plot would, in the linear advance of the text (which therefore, like any novel, should be read in sequence) . . . grows by the variational development of the characters who progress, not in the time-groove and localized space expressive of certain cant assumptions of our dying culture, but in accord with the development of the Theme as it must grow in life: from unconsciousness toward whole, ecstatic knowledge."[2]

The unifying theme is revealed, according to Frank, in the three quotations printed as mottoes for the book which are in combination an idea of Heaven and Hell. The lines from Marlowe, and the source of the title of the novel, suggest that "WHEN ALL THE WORLD DISSOLVES, AND EVERY CREATURE SHALL BE PURIFIED, ALL PLACES SHALL BE HELL THAT IS NOT HEAVEN." The words of Jesus, quoted from *Luke*, place this "heaven" within each man: "The kingdom of God cometh not with observation . . . . the kingdom of God is within you." If man does not find that Heaven, he remains in Hell, where, in the words of St. Catherine of Genoa, "Nothing burns in Hell but the Self."

Thus the stories, being variations upon a theme, constitute a novel about the "hell" of human life from which the quality of "heaven" is excluded; and the unity of the narrative, as Frank points out in "An Aside," is deeper than that of place, being "the attempted unity of each episode's passional crisis, which joins the characters beyond the separate cells of their lives, and merges them upon a common Ground of consciousness and revelation . . . . to the eternal Ground, active within them, whose dimensions both within and beyond time-space inevitably locate the characters by different coordinates than the flat ones of conventional fiction."

The theme is first stated obversely in the Prelude, "Antient History," a satirical, allegorical fantasy depicting the absurdity of trying to find a satisfactory life through changes in externals only. The tremendous popular success of an obscure artist's paintings of simple, familiar scenes in which everyone is nude leads to the banning of clothing throughout the world. Nudity eliminates most of the vanities of life and diverts the technology of civilization to the creation of atomic heating plants instead of bombs. The ironic effect of a return to Eden, however, is a widespread boredom that gives rise to all manner of outrages. Chaos is temporarily checked by the crusade of a young technician to make his disgruntled fellows realize that God is *in* the flesh that they now despise and that only consciousness of this God within each person can cure the disease of weariness and corruption. On the Public Forum of the Air, he says, "*For if He lives in us, He the creator of Cosmos, Cosmos lives in us*; and how, with the power that drives and keeps the suns upon their courses, could we be weary?"

But, when the young prophet talks himself to death in a few years, his interpreters spawn controversy, contention, and combat until the sect of The Pure force a return to clothes as an act of God: "God is hidden; this is the one positive fact man knows of Him. Therefore, to hide Him becomes the one act to express Him." The nations return to manufacturing clothes, patriotism, and war; and each man is once again left to find God in himself.

In the twelve "variations" on this theme, the characters move progressively closer to an awareness of God within them. In the first four stories the awareness is too twisted or superficial to release the protagonists from their private hells. "The Sandwich Man" shows a Bowery bum, unable to adjust to the opportunity to resume the life that he has fled, going mad in the delusion that he has become an instrument of God's power to destroy men capriciously. "The Merits of the Fathers," more an attack on loveless marriages than an echo of the unifying theme, tells of the twisted sexuality created in the children of a union nurtured only by indifference and hatred. In "A Jar of Syrup," a prim, officious spinster, whose antipathy for sugar symbolizes her rigid rationalism, is driven crazy by the irrationality of love, as inexplicable as God's, which is manifest in the anonymous gift of a jar of maple syrup. In "The Last Word," which completes Part One, husband and wife are self-centered and empty; God is only an expletive in their lives; and their mutual inadequacies drive them to a kind of destructive violence expressed in loveless sex.

"The Red Sea," a fantasy about a Negro Moses who supposedly led a band of slaves through the Gulf to freedom, is, in Frank's words in Notebook XIX, "the penultimate statement: . . . ecstasy, seeming salvation *through* illusion: life is lived but not consciously accepted." The narrator, who thinks that he saw the Negro exodus while he was sailing near Barbados, observes, when told that his illusion is a folk tale, that "man can't stand a toothache, but the mystery of life he carries along with ease." Another mystery of life is portrayed in the next story, "One Happy Marriage," which offers an ironic counterpoint to the unhappy unions in the novel. A supremely contented married couple come to realize that their relationship has no meaning because they have none as persons. "Perfect harmony also secretes poison—if it is harmony in any whole less than God," Frank observes in the notebook.

What Frank is trying to say in these stories is most clearly revealed in Notebook XIX in a passage written as he searched for "a continuity-principle, an organic nucleus" which would justify his trying to develop his fourteen plot ideas as a novel:

> As they stand, pale and vague in my mind (and in my notebooks) they are episodes, scarce worth writing. Somehow, I want to fit them into the Modern Tragedy, to make them bespeak and reveal it. These frustrated people whose path, equally if it be of good or of ill will, comes to *personal* disaster——what truth of our times do they articulate? What gave these episodes, noted-down independently through years, their implicit unity? Man is not to be separated from his matrix——the dynamic forms of his times. And yet he *never* fits in. Never! Hence the almost irresistible proneness of all cultures toward some kind of transcendentalism ——the need to fit-in *otherwise*, since neither joy nor success nor contentment is adequate to the human situation. Behind ugliness of failure, always beauty; behind happiness & beauty, ugliness & heartbreak; behind justice injustice, and injustice revealing justice. The interminable dialectic of human pathos. Implicit, not

too obviously, I want to reveal the signature of our time in these tales: the time of a Hitler as Fuehrer, of totalitarian strong-arm communists as bearers of social-justice, of industrialism's gas chamber, of the Church of Christ collaborating with war-mongers, of the irony of Palestine, of hysterically scared America, et al. . . .

One terrible truth of the times is exposed in "The Humanitarian," the seventh variation on the over-all metaphysical theme. In it, the dedicated exponent of Christ's teachings elects to go lower and lower in the economic and social world instead of compromising in the slightest; but, like so many fervent Christians all over the world, he becomes an impotent bystander when racial violence strikes down the one man, a Jew, who loved and respected him.

Almost perversely, Frank returns to the intensely personal in the remaining variations; but the eighth, "Culture of the West," is an oblique criticism of rigid sexual mores. In it, spinster sisters, incipient lesbians, plunge into the ocean clasping each other when the normal sexual experience of one threatens to separate them. "The Cat," which opens the third group of variations, tells of the effort of a disillusioned young Bostonian to isolate himself from the world. But he adopts a stray kitten and in a couple of years discovers through the cat that he is trying to escape his mean averageness. He wishes to make his relationship with the animal something deeper to correspond to his own tumultuous feeling; in his bitter disappointment in "the skin of separateness" he sees in the enigmatic eyes of the cat, he throws the animal from him. Its body strikes the corner of a table. When it dies, he returns to the hated family bank to accept his form of the average by becoming an office boy for life. He attempts to explain his motivation to his unsympathetic uncle: "What moves us all, who are the norm, to get beyond the norm? Some through delusions of grandeur; some by possessing a personal god, nation, race; some in dream . . . ; some in swinishness, destruction; if all else fails, in self-destruction? What moves us beyond us? The Mover who is in us. It's not belief I'm talking about, it's a presence."

"A Man Who Loved Children" reveals the "presence" also through the animal world. A sea captain returns from a voyage to find his beloved wife dead and his infant an idiot. He dedicates his life to the child, however, when it responds to a mongrel who jumps up at them: "His eyes, deep with tenderness, that amusingly contrasted with his shrill bark and skinny body all out of kilter with the wagging tail. . . ." Another story, "Samson," reiterates the idea that one must lose his life to find it. The head of a prospering family, having decided that the American dream destroys awareness and love, deliberately bankrupts himself; but, when he then discovers that his children are still capable of love, he starts again. The last variation, appropriately titled "Victory," pictures a similar life-restoring sacrifice. A child of nature finds love; and her foster father, whose incestuous lust has been indirectly responsible for the girl's blindness, finds peace in devoting himself to her care. When he is certain that she will no longer need him, he speeds his dying. As his neighbors carry his pine coffin to the crest of a hill, "suddenly it tried to soar. . . . Over the crest . . . the coffin was light, as if empty."

But these are only variations on the theme; in them, the Self burns in the Hell of life, permitting a mere glimpse of Heaven to those who do not achieve it. The last story, "The Kingdom of Heaven," sounds the theme, which "is ecstasy, salvation, grace, through Acceptance of life's horror: [and] rejection of all illusion" in contrast to "salvation *through* illusion." The plot of "The Kingdom of Heaven" is minimal: a young Argentinian poet, who has been an active revolutionist, is captured by the *caudillo*, who elects a more exquisite punishment than shooting for the author of the brash attack on him in *A Pampa Tiger*. Stripped naked, Juan is tightly bound and sewn securely, only his head free, in the skin of a freshly killed steer; then the bundle, looking like "a huge cocoon," is carried into the pampa and placed so that Juan's face is to the sun. The rest of the story is a detailed account of his excruciating agony during the endless three days and two nights he survives. But the horror is that of the Book of Job rather than of "The Pit and the Pendulum." It is prolonged in order to create the ecstasy, the transcendent illumination, that is all one can know of Heaven.

Since this idea is basic to Frank's concept of the Whole, it is not surprising to find that he saw its place in this story when he first sketched it in 1929. He writes an explanation in Notebook X:

> The tale is devoted to the description of his battle . . . to *tolerate* his situation & to *harmonize* it with his mystical sense of the Whole. . . . He accepts & feels harmony & wholeness. Pain does not go but becomes detached. Fear goes & hate and rebellion. To achieve it, he has had to reject a personal God & Christ.

> (For how would this lot be tolerable . . . to one who had never heard of Christ? It must be universally acceptable within a whole, else it is not acceptable at all).
>
> As he achieves fulness of understanding & complete objective acceptance of the body & its fate, death comes to him—merged into a physical detachment & a spiritual release.

Near the end Juan calls to God and the *caudillo*, now "a bearded vulture," appears in a vision to mock him:

> "What is this God of yours?" asked the red eyes. "He gives you nerves to torture you; pride to humiliate you; dreams and a heart in order to break them; life in order to kill. . . . A clever cruel son-of-bitch, your God. Don't contradict me."
>
> "I don't."
>
> "So you agree?"
>
> "That's your part of the truth. Fly away and wait for it."

The mirage vanishes; but from the silence within Juan, instead of from the whirlwind, comes forth a voice: "God!" and "Juan saw himself standing . . . alone in the pampa . . . . suspended in the tension of two poles: one, huge, parabolic, the world unto the stars; one, dimensionless, within him. . . . He lay on his back, and his eyes saw the eyes of the vultures. He stood. . . ." He has sensed in the pain of his torture the mystic presence, the kingdom of heaven within himself. He has not been carried up to Heaven because of his suffering; he has found salvation through the acceptance of whatever is "not Heaven" and his soul has stood erect.

These are original, highly symbolic tales of considerable power, which would be almost meaningless as independent stories. Therefore, they must be considered a cycle if not a novel; and, in view of the rapidly changing concepts of the novel in this century, it seems pedantic to deny use of the term. But this critical latitude makes comparative evaluation of the volume difficult, if not impossible. Obviously, *Not Heaven* cannot be discussed in terms of the conventional novel or short story, and comparison with other story cycles would appear to be unenlightening. The problem is a tribute to Frank's creative imagination, which is, perhaps, the most impressive feature of *Not Heaven.* It enables Frank to project philosophical and religious abstractions through the Naturalistic details of his fiction in an interesting and challenging—if not always convincing—manner. He once described himself, in Notebook IX, as a "realistic mystic," a contradiction exemplified in his fiction and justified by his objective: "I propose by my activity to generate cosmic knowledge and divine vision *within* the human domain—not, as in many religious activities employ this impulse to know as an incentive to escape." This rationale for his fictions relegates esthetic judgments to the limitations of relative taste or to impressionistic criticism.

III *The Jews Today*

Following the publication of *Not Heaven*, Frank turned to the preparations of a philosophical statement of the views expressed symbolically in his fiction. Work on *The Rediscovery of Man* in turn stimulated a resumption of critical and political journalism, which led to an agreement in April, 1954, to write monthly a syndicated column, "Voz de America," for thirty Latin American papers. The column gave Frank an excuse and a commission to visit Israel in 1956 to do a series of articles on the Jewish state. In writing the series, he came to realize that he had "something other to say: something more direct in the sense of Israel's relation, and the Jews', with history and with man." So he expanded the largely factual articles into a book, *Bridgehead: The Drama of Israel* (1957).

Although Frank admits in Notebook XXVI that he regards the book as "impressionistic" rather than "*personal*," in the sense that *Virgin Spain* and *America Hispana* were "personal," its theme is his familiar one of the Person, the People, and the Cosmos. Israel is obviously a bridgehead of the West in the Middle East: "The Jew in his overriding ethicism represents the dynamic West" in its struggle with pragmatic Islam; and it is the Jew's opportunity, as well as responsibility, to effect Arab-Israeli understanding: "cosmic vision is needed, and cosmic vision transcends the 'practical' and transforms it."[3]

The vision, Frank warns, may be lost in the increasing self-absorption and self-sufficiency of the Israeli. Frank sees the kibbutz producing "collective individuals" instead of "collective persons." But "when the self discovers and develops its share of the Cosmic, the *individual* becomes a *person*"; then he can express his cosmic relationship in meaningful social terms. If the Israelis lose "that specific consciousness of relationship with Cosmos," which marks the strength and genius of history, they will have sacrificed identity for existence. "The survival of the Jew has hinged on his prophetic sense of brotherhood with all men, inclusive of his enemies, under God. His social intelligence flowed from his *aesthetic* of personal relation with the Cosmos. If in his battle to survive . . . he loses this relation, what survives in Palestine will not be Israel . . . not if the name holds its traditional Jewish meaning."

Bridgehead is the book about the Jew which Frank always planned to write but did not succeed in writing in *The Jew in Our Day.* It is not just a loosely joined collection of his journalistic pieces. It employs the facts which went into the articles but only to reveal the drama of a people behind the politics and the economics. From his "impressionistic" description of the "facts" of Israel—geography, cities, arts, leaders—he moves back and forth in history to discover the "forces" defining Jewishness and threatening the Israelis. He looks upon "scenes like instruments of an orchestra, playing a single theme in individual *timbres.*" They portray the "drama of Israel" in graphic, human terms because they are created with and by people in Frank's most relaxed and engratiating style.

The prose in the philosophical sections of the book is naturally more complex and difficult; but it is relieved by the eloquence and sharpness of insight—or challenge—in such passages as this: "The quarrels of the Middle East have blinded participants and spectators to the basic fact that these lands are inhabited by human beings: by men and women and children! If the world can grow aware of this, it will become aware of the rights of these men and women to live; it will be able to impose this awareness upon all the actors of the conflict; and a start will begin out of the marish and nightmarish maze."

In a world of power politics, Frank's point of view is undoubtedly as naïve as the Sermon on the Mount; but his vision nevertheless had some appeal since *Bridgehead* enjoyed an unusual success for a book about Israel despite the fact, according to Bittner, that "nearly every one of the magazines directed at a mainly Jewish readership reviewed it very adversely."[4] Frank's candid rejection both of Zionism and of hostility toward the Arab probably explains the critical reviews; perhaps the less partisan reader responds to the world view evident in such a simple premise as this: "If Jerusalem became one city of God—of God worshiped in the similitudes of Catholic, Protestant, Mohammedan and Jew—our world might become one city of man."

CHAPTER *11*

Rediscovering Man

THE TRIP TO ISRAEL and the writing of *Bridgehead* were merely interludes in the four years of intensive labor which Frank expended on *The Rediscovery of Man: A Memoir and a Methodology of Modern Life.* He finished it late in August, 1957, and immediately returned to fiction, drafting a novel, *A Regular Fella.* He also lectured in Guatemala and wrote a long essay on Mexico for a collection of studies of that country.

I *Group Dynamics*

A proposed subtitle for *The Rediscovery of Man,* recorded in Frank's journal, is more descriptive of the objective of the book than the one used: "An Inquiry into the Nature of the Person in Terms of American Life." For in this work Frank tries to go beyond the conclusions of his novels which reveal the process by which a character becomes a Person but do not show how the Person then copes with a world of chaos and hate. Frank announces in the first sentence of the Introduction that "the purpose of this book is to suggest a method for living in the modern world—not an exclusive or dogmatic method, but one which will move the reader toward developing his own."[1] Frank is the protagonist whose search for a method for living constitutes the "Memoir" of the book: the account of "a life recording its stages by the ideas which have moved it."

This study of Frank and his works is not the place to attempt a detailed analysis of this long, dense, philosophical statement of the author's concept of the Person; but the general nature and method of the book can be indicated without detracting unfairly from the richness of the knowledge and the challenge of the vision in this call to greatness. Book I is largely descriptive, being a history of the development of the individual instead of the Person in the Western world after the Renaissance. Beginning with what Frank calls a "Spectrograph of European Man," the book traces the birth of modern Western man in the individual: one who "acts in this life as if his self were indivisible, autonomous, discrete, and assumes that other selves have the same nature . . . . but his basic principle of reference remains *his* independence, his individual will." In an increasingly powerful circle, this man's "ego absorbs the cosmic to itself; the cosmic makes the ego strong, and the stronger, the more demonic." The result is that science supplants sacrament; technology replaces revelation.

As the organic synthesis of Christian knowledge faded, the new faiths brightened: "Humanism, Protestantism, nationalism, and the successes of science . . . subtly at first, soon sweepingly and openly, spoiled the soundness of the constituents of the living and lived Christian drama." Rabelais, Shakespeare, Cervantes, Milton, Racine, Pascal, Montaigne, and Swift graphically portray the growth of the individual, huge as Gargantua, and as animalistic as the Yahoo. Ferments within Europe's sacramental culture gradually corrode, however; and the subsequent search for compensatory powers takes the dominant forms of faith and of experimental science. "Nature replaced the cosmic Presence"; the machine replaces the sacrament, "above all in the United States."

The movement of the West since 1600 away from a culture based "upon the *knowledge* of the Presence of God within empirical reality, to a civilization of *faith* in empirical information and its laws," falls into three phases: first, sacramentalism persists but faith is increasingly stressed; second, in an age of romantic revolutions, "the sacrament is transformed or deliberately set aside in favor of the revelations of nature, the sufficiency of reason, or in favor of the ego . . . as the sole locus of truth"; and third, mechanism is endowed with sacramental powers, ushering in the age of American business and of Russian Communism, or "Man with Mechanism" and "Man under Mechanism." Therefore, "because both systems lacked knowledge and method for coping with the human ego, individual and collective, their machines, both technical and social, were run and over-run by ego. Ego is the converging State, capitalist and Communist."

Between these two giant states, which threaten to destroy the world, the majority of mankind cowers, inwardly rejecting both militant mechanisms. In a generation or two, these frightened peoples will control the mass of the world's resources; and, if they have not already been corrupted by the egocentric power complex of Western civilization, they may find a leadership in Asia or in Latin America which will guide them to a realization of the potential in the Person. If the West, on the other hand, decides that it wishes to escape the cultural death implicit in mechanization, it will have to make a start by renouncing Positivism, which ignores the Person and creates "a pseudo-universe of *parts*, from which the self with its intuitive sense of its whole nature is crowded out." If man is to save himself from a world now threatened by atomic and biological explosions, he must develop an instinct which will enable him to use science to discover his place instead of surrendering to science.

In Book II, Frank leaves descriptive anthropology, by which he has tried to find accepted in history, as a value, "the people's sense, individual and collective, of relation with life," for a journey into psychology in an effort to "*establish* this relation as value, its consciousness as value, by exposing it as a basic constant of man's nature." The theme of this book is the nature of revelation, which is analyzed in terms of the function and knowledge of man's relation with the whole of Being; of the dimensions of the self, of Cosmos, of God; and, finally, of the potential of psychology as a method of action.

Man's *conscious* knowledge of his relation with the whole of Being is a necessary value which affords a clarification of man's nature, past and present, and is a guide to his future. "It is this book's business to show that the datum of revelation is here and is within us" and that "the individual's true potential" is the Person. The next step is "to define the cosmic presence as psychologically and logically real" by finding traces of transcendence in man's psychological forms—such as love, art, language, beauty—which go beyond mere relations of function toward articulations of the knowledge of their direct relation with Being. Then these traces must be brought into focus in order to provide a fulcrum for methodological action once the true dimensions of man—the self—are established and known.

To the two dimensions of man—the ego and the group—which for most schools of psychology constitute the whole of the self, Frank now adds "the cosmic dimension," the continuum linking all things:

> It is a harmony of man's empirical relations. His work, his love, his needs and aspirations, all individually within the group and ego dimensions, create an overtone which transcends them. This is the "spiritual," and it is universally human. What men call the

> good, and no less the evil; the divine, and no less the profane; both love and hate, faith and anxiety, are evidences of spirit. Every man who breathes partakes of it, although more often in deprivation and failure than fulfillment—whence his recognition of the tragic in history and in his nature.

The variants of the mixture of the three dimensions are responsible for the differences in cultures and individuals. Of the five types of self, Frank is concerned primarily with the fifth, the one in which the cosmic dimension nurtures the Person and the groups of Persons by controlling the ego and group dimensions:

> The person is the individual whose functions, included in the broad realms of the group and ego dimensions, are not suppressed, not distorted, and not dominant; but are constantly, inwardly, informed by his sense of the whole self in which the cosmic is an active vector. This person will eat, play, love, follow a trade, have friends and enemies, predilections and aversions; suffer joy and pain, defeats and victories, fight for causes or against them—all within the pattern of his culture and within groups of similarly centered persons. But each of his acts, expressing a function of relation with his somatic ego and his group, will be suffused and transfigured by his experience of the whole, not as exterior cosmos but as cosmic quality within him; tincturing his empiric emotion and thought, yet beyond them; formed as space-time, yet beyond it. *The person is the individual made real.*

Book III presents Frank's psychological method for creating the Person from the individual by "socio-integration" and "psycho-integration." The first is concerned with the development of organic groups in place of merely organized ones. Frank analyzes major groups in American life both in terms of what they are and what they might be; the most significant of these groupings are represented by (1) sex and marriage, (2) school and church, (3) labor and management, (4) minorities, (5) economy, and (6) artist and enjoyer. As these groups become more organized in the culture, they become less organic, less aware of the cosmic. For instance, what is good for General Motors is not necessarily good for the American people, except, of course, in a purely material sense. And the same thing can be said of labor: "The American labor union's concept of itself is largely organizational, not organic. Its cultural contribution has been paltry. Where its sense of welfare goes beyond physical health, it has slavishly followed conventional creeds. It has produced no thinkers, no artists, hardly a respectable critic of itself. Its relations with the creative minds of the community at large have been without imagination. It can propose programs for specific tactical ends; it has no roots for creative strategy." It follows that there is discontinuity between the values of the self as established in family or school and in economic or political groups.

Frank believes that this discontinuity could be abolished through the development of some kind of guild syndicalism: "Each such group will be like an organ, and as the cells within the organ collaborate to form it, the economic organs of the community will collaborate to form the whole body politic; while it, as a whole, nourishes the organs, the cells, the whole body feeding its parts and distributing the oxygen of life through the bloodstream." But, like the biological organism, each social group must have some ego-denying principle, some form of cosmic knowledge which will hold development to the nomative pattern. In social groups, this knowledge must be conscious; hence the imperative need is for groups of Persons, who alone can make socio-integration possible.

Psycho-integration, on the other hand, is Frank's term for a method of inducing cosmic awareness within the self: the mystical revelation which permits and inspires the development of the Person beyond the individual. He gives only a general sketch of the method in Book III, reserving for the Appendices a description of his psychological technique and a collection of his original notes on the process of revelation as he understands it.

The Rediscovery of Man is an impressive summation of Frank's philosophy and faith, an intellectual memoir which, as he admits in Appendix B, he hopes may "also be a summons." For everything remains to be done: "This book is the barest notation. The most effective work may not at first be visible at all. It will be vastly varied; thousands of men and women in multiple idioms and places will be engaged in it, are engaged in it already. Like the cells multiplying, differentiating, joining, each at its task of creating man's organic body."

Thus, psycho-integration points toward the future and the restoration of revelation as a force. If the world of tomorrow is to have any religion, it may have to create one within the postulates defined in this book. And, even if man should fail to develop his cosmic dimension through Frank's version of group dynamics, he will at least have experienced the enrichment of discovering a tragic vision. "We move into an era of unprecedented freedom," Frank proclaims in the ringing tones of the Hebrew prophets of old. "We are free to destroy, free to create. . . . The time of Man begins."

II *Political Revolution*

After the publication of *The Rediscovery of Man*, Frank went to Southern France in November, 1958, to work on revisions of the new novel, *A Regular Fella*; he returned to New York in March of the next year and then journeyed to Mexico in May to act as a judge in a novel-writing competition. Late in the summer, one of his *Voz* articles, a fanciful piece on the conference of the Organization of American States in Chile, attracted such favorable notice in the Havana press that Frank was invited to visit Cuba as a friend of the revolution. This invitation set in motion a chain of events which led to the composition and publication, after some very trying circumstances, of the last book which Frank published, *Cuba: Prophetic Island.*

Frank visited Cuba in the fall of 1959 and was urged by Amando Hart Davalos, the minister of education, and Chancellor Raul Roa, chairman of the office of cultural relations, to write the story of Cuba. At the same time, Prensa Latina, a pro-Castro news agency, asked Frank to become a regular weekly contributor; but he rejected this offer in order to avoid adding another journalistic deadline to his working schedule, which would undoubtedly interfere with the writing of another novel.

From December until March, 1960, Frank worked on the rough draft of a novel about high-priced "call girls," which he entitled *Cleopatra Madden.* He also made notes for a book of memoirs while he waited for the Cuban government to send him a contract for the proposed book about the island. As friction between the State Department and Castro increased, Frank became Temporary Chairman of the Fair Play for Cuba Committee; but he was beginning to have doubts about Castro. "His hysterical speeches sicken me," he admitted in his journal; and then he wondered: "If he opposed an action would he inevitably modulate from opposition to violence?"

Increasingly impatient to have some decision from the Cubans, Frank used the occasion of a conference of intellectuals in Havana at the end of April to go to the island to get a contract to do the book for his price of twenty-five thousand dollars. He spent the remainder of the summer working on a draft, but the writing was difficult because of his deepening concern over Castro's dictatorial behavior. Frank talked to himself in Notebook XXVI: "I undertook to write my book on Cuba with exactly *one* implied proviso: that my response to Cuba & its Revolution was positive and favorable (not necessarily uncritical.). . . . Well, now, I am *not* absolutely sure that I approve of the Government-trends, . . . those of a dictator . . . . [but] they by no means stultify the assignment." He decided to make the book personal in the way that *Virgin Spain* and *America Hispana* are personal instead of impressionistic like *Bridgehead* or a systematic portrait like the study of Bolivar.

He resigned his Chairmanship of the Fair Play for Cuba Committee, but he continued as a member of that organization. He objected to the policy of the State Department toward Castro because he saw it as one that would drive Castro into the willing arms of the Russians. A journal entry clearly states Frank's attitude as of August, 1960: "Castro is right to do business with the Com[munist] countries; he is right in saying that professional anti-C[ommunism] is (almost wholly) counter-revolutionary. He is right to devote all his time, as he does, to his magnificent Revolution. But he should make clear, where—–ideologically—– he differs from Communism. Point is, as Sartre said, he has no theory, no ideology, strictly speaking: he *acts*, & when he talks it is not well."

Following Castro's appearance at the United Nations, Frank returned to Cuba to interview the leaders in the revolution. He had dinner and a three-hour conversation with Castro, after which he wrote in his journal: "Fidel in great shape. He is a genius & he may be mad." Frank remained in Cuba nearly a month; and, when he returned to New York at the end of October, he had completed a rough draft of the book. But only Beacon Press was willing to consider publishing it, although Losada in Buenos Aires accepted it enthusiastically after seeing only the "Prelude."

Unfortunately, Frank did not inform Beacon of the fee that he had received from the Cuban government for writing the book; and, when the General Council of the Unitarian Church, which owns the press, learned of the grant, it refused to honor the contract, claiming that Frank had in effect invalidated it by his silence. Meanwhile, the failure of the attempted invasion of Cuba and Frank's subsequent published criticism of that attempt further complicated his situation. Congressional hearings on the

Fair Play for Cuba Committee in June evoked numerous references to Frank's political affiliations and activities; moreover, his 1932 statement in the *New Masses*, "How I Came to Communism," was published as an appendix to the report of the hearings, although he was not called to testify. (The Committee on Un-American Activities summoned him in 1962 to appear at an executive session, at which he was questioned some three and a half hours; and he also testified before the Senate Internal Security Committee on March 8, 1963.)

In view of the general hostility toward Castro in the spring of 1961, Frank's behavior in his dealings with Beacon Press was incredibly naïve, as he later realized. A notebook entry about a week before Beacon's final decision to ignore the contract indicates the rationalizations responsible for Frank's naïveté: "I feel guilty! and yet I knew with my whole mind that I did nothing wrong. . . . But I could have known—as Cuban conditions worsened, that what I did would *seem* wrong . . . be *judged* as wrong by 'people'. . . . I feared they would hesitate to take the book—which is likely. So I played a game of silence—and this is what hurts me, now: although *I* knew—& my Cuban sponsors know that what I accepted to do the job was essentially as proper as my grant from the Bollingen Foundation [to write *The Rediscovery of Man*] or from Venezuela to write my Bolivar. . . ." It is, of course, ironic that Frank's desire for publication should trap him in the kind of pragmatic logic denounced in all his books; but his experience also underscores the validity of his criticism of that kind of reasoning.

Fortunately, Frank's work on the book was not lost; a newly formed publishing firm, Marzani and Munsell, was glad to get the manuscript, and *Cuba: Prophetic Island* was published in October, 1961. But by that time the circumstances of its inception were known, and Castro had admitted his Communist ties. As a result, the book received little notice; and this understandable reaction is regrettable. For Frank's study, which includes the political and economic history of the troubled island, puts the current crisis in its proper perspective and affords a useful portrayal of the ambivalent relations of Cuba and the United States. It also reveals the reasons for the popularity of Castro and his revolution. Frank gives Castro the full benefit of his own personal doubts and hopes; he rationalizes too many of the weaknesses of the revolution and its leader; but he admits his concern over Castro's temperament and political inclinations. Like most friends of Cuba, Frank later deplored Castro's betrayal of the revolution; but the Cuban leader's defection does not invalidate the need for that revolution or for the world's understanding of it. And Frank's book makes these two important considerations clear.

In the book Frank uses a non-linear treatment of themes and events to exploit the sensuous and the philosophic elements in his view of the history and the culture of Cuba in order to give a sense of Cuba instead of just statistics. The Prelude brings Castro on stage at the United Nations; Frank then switches to the history of Cuba during the nineteenth century and to the contribution of Jose Marti, the "Saint with a Sword" who represents for Frank the true Person who realizes his total self in social action. The portrait drawn of Marti is an especially sensitive and illuminating one, a miniature of the larger canvas of Bolivar. The next section, "The Face of Revolutionary Cuba," develops theme in terms of place: in Havana, long alienated by its character from the rest of the country, Batista's yacht club is now a dance hall for workers; in Cienfuegos and Trinidad, in Pinar del Rio and Viñales, the present takes its harsh, uneven forms; but "the change is always for man: from submission to creation."[2] In Matanzas, a black molten human mass flowing around Castro acts out a ritual embrace which Frank assumes that no dictator could inspire. In Santiago, the grim Moncada Barracks symbolize the wild vision and reckless courage of the men who built a successful revolution out of an initial disaster.

After the dramatic account of Castro's early failure at Moncada Barracks, Frank resumes a contrapuntal presentation of the history of Cuba set against the "Blood and Irony" of America's political manipulation of the island from the time of Adams and Jefferson until Castro's seizure of power. In this sordid tale of exploitation Cuba is repeatedly betrayed by both its suppressors and supposed liberators—just as the citizens of the United States, who had openly expressed their desire for freedom for the Cubans, were betrayed by their countrymen's manipulation of Cuba for commercial gain. "McKinley believed in the Cubans' right to liberty; and no less in the right of American business . . . to do what it wanted to do in Cuba. . . . The convictions incarnate in McKinley summed to ambiguity and to the hypocrisy of trying to rationalize, justify and preserve the contradictions. They characterize the American state policy toward Cuba from that day forward."

In a chapter entitled "Methods and Men," Frank analyzes, sympathetically yet critically, the difficulties of effective reform in Cuba and the personalities of the reformers who have tried to reform it, including Fidel Castro. Frank's candidly expressed reservations about the methods and the men support his indignant rejection of the role of hired propagandist. He warns Castro, for example, that nationalization of industries must not be an end in itself, since nationalization does not automatically equate with true socialization of production and usually creates a new form of bureaucracy which can be quite as retarding as the one it replaces. Frank is also suspicious of what he calls "romanticism" in any revolution, and he can only hope that the Cuban rebels will prove equal to the "complexity of reform." His generally favorable portrait of the Cuban leader has the darker colors of his doubts and fears:

> The outstanding, the frightening trait of Fidel Castro is, of course, his rejection of gradualism. . . .
>
> . . . . He is not a meditative, not a contemplative man. . . . Although not without culture and mental training, Castro is not therefore an intellectual. . . . But in his exquisite sensibilities and responsiveness to every live detail around him, he is less the politician than the poet. . . .
>
> . . . . To call him a "dictator" is dishonest semantics. He writes down in deed what Cuba's needs dictate. But, as he is the most conspicuous Hispano-American leader of our time, he is also the most exposed to jeopardy, from without and within himself. As a man of genius, he of course identifies his self with the substance of his work. But if the identification becomes possessive, he will no longer be the good leader. The great question about Fidel Castro is whether he has enough intellectual detachment to recognize in himself the evils of the lusting ego, which he shares with all men and which might distort his vision and stultify his uses.

Because Castro is not a meditative man, Frank is especially troubled by his seeming response to the "mass mind," by the "direct, almost physical embrace of leaders and people." Politics, as Frank sees it, must be related to the psychology which makes possible the "rediscovery of man," instead of the release of the mob, to be productive of good. If the Cuban revolution, for example, is to achieve more than an exchange of oppressors of the people, "there must be a return to the self, an *education* of the self, not imagined today in such crude ideologies as the orthodox materialism of the Communists or the orthodox rationalism of the capitalists or the nationalisms now rampant in many parts of the world."

The last scene in the book is an amusing, somewhat pathetic, one in which a weary old man scolds Castro and his shouting comrades for making sleep impossible. At the end of a long, exhausting day of inspecting swamp-drainage projects with Castro, seventy-two-year-old Frank falls into his bunk at midnight in the headquarters building of the drainage engineers while the rest of the inspecting party continues to eat, drink, and argue, in a way which reminds Frank of "jam sessions at college." Awakened suddenly at three o'clock in the morning, by "prolific shouting," Frank angrily pads into the next room to rebuke Castro and his companions for disturbing "the old man who needs his sleep, the good-hearted Yankee." The offenders, including Castro, offer apologies sheepishly; and Frank returns to his bunk. Next day, however, he awakens to full awareness of his impertinence in daring to rebuke Castro, especially in public, and now Frank is ready to apologize; but Castro does not mention the incident, and Frank realizes that he does not really know much about Castro the man.

The episode symbolizes Waldo Frank's point of view in the book. He is the uneasy yet hopeful parent desperately trying to understand and support an unruly, impetuous offspring. With patience and love he tries to believe in the essential goodness of his young rebel, to give him the benefit of his doubts, hoping thereby to nurture the necessary development of the whole man, the Person, who will in his social actions justify the bright promise of his youth. Like every parent, Frank is too ready to overlook, or rationalize, the young man's mistakes and weaknesses; but hindsight makes his tolerance and faith appear more naïve in 1967 than they were in fact in 1960. Frank was not alone in his acceptance of Castro's denial of party membership; and ultimately his distress over Castro's betrayal of the revolution was deeper and greater than that of most Cuban sympathizers because of the intensity and duration of Frank's love affair with America Hispana.

Frank was wrong about Castro, but that error of judgment does not invalidate the usefulness of a book that puts Cuba vividly before the reader and conveys movingly the sad plight of the Cubans. As Frank says in the last sentence of his text, "Consciousness of what the Cubans are today must become the premise of American collaboration in what the Cubans are doing." *Cuba: Prophetic Island* informs the consciousness, preparing it for what should be an inevitable collaboration.

III *Unfinished Business*

Although the book on Cuba was to be Frank's last publication, he continued, despite his discouragement over the rejection of *A Regular Fella* by a dozen publishers, to work at his writing. *A Regular Fella* is an attempt at a depth portrait of a man to reveal the ephemeral surface of all ethic. Frank describes it in his working notes as "an exercise in antinomianism. . . . Character is articulated simply, dynamically as existential foliation of being. *Being* is the story. Each character with an unconscious shrewdness turns events into expressions of self. Thus, P. is masochist, Felice is power-hungry altruist—E. is pure Being almost void of existence (even his words are non-communicative)."

To some publishers, the novel seemed old-fashioned, probably because Frank returned for its structure to his earliest "lyric novels." "The *surfaces* . . the continuity of intricately varied events, are lyrically presented. . . . Underlying all, the beat & rhythm of M's will—which is the American will: to succeed. As this proceeds, M. negates or, rather, opposes it . . *sabotages* it with his basic masochism, which is a paritive *anti-success*."

Frank also continued to work on the manuscript of *Cleopatra Madden*, a novel whose theme and structure are comparable to those of *A Regular Fella*. This tale of a schoolteacher who doubles as a high-priced "call girl" is meant to be a satiric blast at the commercialization of every part of life in the United States: "Schizophrenia & *lack of opportunity*—unemployment of value—are the theme of our America." May Madden, shaped by her dream fantasies into a modern Cleopatra, is pictured as the victim of a schizoid society, as is her potential benefactor, Felix Marr, who has a vague sense of cosmic beauty but finds no social dimension of it. Felix is the last of that long line of self-destroying, satanic males in Frank's novels that started with Tom Rennard in *The Dark Mother*. He cannot save May because of his incompleteness as an individual.

This modern parable is a sordid one that will probably have even less appeal than *A Regular Fella* for publishers. Frank himself wonders openly in his workbook as to the reasons why he is "drawn to a tale of vice, rot, and ugliness" for what was to be his last novel. His recorded answer is that he is compelled by "*the irony* of our successful civilization equated by human wreckage.——the down turning of anxiety & aspiration into sex orgy & money-grabbing, when the cosmic is excised from man's consciousness.——specifically, the ironic endings of both Victorian & modern values——so that the wild night reveals only lost souls, having no answer but a clumsy court sentence of '90 days.' " Although his theme is a valid and important one, Frank was not able to bring it to life, largely because he did not speak the language of this underside of America. Despite his conscientious efforts to learn "jive" talk and to become "hep," his dialogue remains highly self-conscious, artificial, and wholly unconvincing. Frank could neither hear nor feel this dark world.

Although Frank persisted in his hope for some kind of recognition of these two manuscripts, he wisely turned to his own past with a view to mollifying his "demon" by writing his memoirs. Given Frank's long and active career and his talent for social commentary, his personal account of those crucial and dramatic years could have afforded invaluable insights into the social and literary history of the United States in the first half of the century as well as presented a great gallery of portraits of his friends and enemies, most of whom were closely identified with the artistic and political activity of the period. Perhaps in his *Memoir* Frank might have achieved the rediscovery of himself and his writings; indeed, his title for the unwritten Part III of the autobiography is "Death and Birth of Waldo Frank."

CHAPTER 12

What Harvest?

IN 1923 Gorham Munson saw Frank as "the most exciting figure in contemporary American letters . . . . an artist in prose fiction . . . likely to dominate the field in America for a long time."[1] Frank's dominance, however, was short-lived; and he slowly but steadily slid into oblivion in the United States. Today most of his books are out of print and are ignored even by the most ambitious purveyors of reprints.

There can be no definitive explanation of Frank's paradoxical career. Success or failure of an artist is more often a by-product of intangibles, like luck, than evidence of virtue rewarded. The capriciousness of fame is especially trying in the case of a man of letters like Waldo Frank, who had something to say and who said it with verve and color. The literary historian or critic can only guess at the probable causes, but Frank himself believed that his inability to attract a larger or more loyal following in his own country was probably attributable to his diversity as a writer. In a strikingly candid analysis of his "public position," written in Notebook IX in 1928, Frank said of himself: "Each portion of his work, superficially separate from other portions, had won a certain audience for him. . . . But the public so won were separate: neither he nor an integrating power in any appreciable group of readers had organized his image & influence into a whole."

For example, *Our America*, once hailed as "the Manifesto of the Twenties," had by 1928 been silenced by the more raucous voices of the Mencken school of social commentary. The "lyric novels," which had made Frank known to another audience as a literary radical, had never been understood with much clarity or depth,[2] with the consequence that, when he published no fiction for over a decade, he lost even that small audience to more dramatic novelists like Joyce, Fitzgerald, Hemingway, Lewis, and Dos Passos.[3]

Frank's move into social criticism after the early novels, on the other hand, won him still another group of readers: the youths who had never read *Our America* or the novels and the academic liberals who, if they had read his fiction, probably disapproved of it—these two groups applauded the Waldo Frank of the crusading *New Republic.* But their enthusiasm did not embrace the kind of social history soon offered in *Virgin Spain.* In the quoted self-analysis, Frank remarks on the indifference of these groups to the study of Spain: "To the radicals, it committed the sin of taking a Catholic Country seriously: to the 'American culturists' it seemed an escape . . . . an isolated literary excursion." The book had, however, a relatively favorable press; and it created more individual enthusiasms than perhaps any other single work of Frank's. But it did not appreciably identify the writer or his career to the readers in the United States, although it established Frank in America Hispana.[4] Consequently, as the 1920's drew to a close, Frank belonged to no school, and no group supported him. He had become a kind of maverick, an outsider; and the image became fixed during the next decades by his oscillations between criticism and fiction and by his political gyrations.

In addition to the separatistic influence of his diversity, Frank may have contributed to the isolation of his "public position" through his critical stance and temper. This view is admittedly an area of pure speculation and inference, but there is in most of the comments on Frank and his work a tone of animosity and hostility which seems to lie outside the range of objective criticism, no matter how impersonal it professes to be. A representative observation is this one: "Mr. Frank makes it easy to laugh at him. The colossal and tasteless egotism . . . is almost beyond belief."[5] But the remark was made in 1943!

In an essay review of Frank's first two novels, published more than twenty years earlier, Frank's close friend and protégé, Paul Rosenfeld, set the tone of personal criticism:

> The acute dislocation in the form of Frank's novels . . . the form which is neither fiction nor confession, but a perplexing jumble of the two, is the result, of course, of a profound and secret irresolution in the mind of the author. . . . What, it seems evident, Frank really wanted to write, was confession. . . . What Frank's little Jehovah wished to have believed, was that it had been

> singled out and elected by Life; that it had been done, out of sheer malice, a great wrong; that it was a thing ruthlessly singled out and sacrificed, one of a generation foredoomed, above all other generations, to failure and nonentity. . . . It would not permit him to confess; for confession, in establishing the truth of the relation between his ego and the egoes of others, would have disproved its claim of fateful distinction. . . .
>
> . . . . For there was in the author an element that denied his very personages. Not only did he refuse to listen to the characters he had proposed himself, and made them see and feel and hear Waldo Frank. He also showed that he considered them negligible. . . .[6]

Munson answered Rosenfeld at length in his *Study*, but later he too turned against Frank.

The 1920's was a period of unusually blunt, vituperative criticism; and Frank was an effective exponent of the style, as already seen in *Salvos* and in *Time Exposures*. In a position of some power and prestige as the active force behind the *Seven Arts*, Frank undoubtedly appeared to many as a bright, precocious young Jew beginning to make his presence felt in the arts, especially in those nurtured in New York. After his mystical experience and "conversion" to Judaism early in 1920, Frank became a self-anointed "prophet" engaged in writing "proofs of God," a stance which by its very presumptions must have annoyed and alienated many tough-minded adherents to the "lost generation." Even Frank admits that his writings before 1928 either puzzled or irritated. Thereafter, they are apt to be received in the spirit of Sidney Hook, who titles his review of *The Rediscovery of America*, "The Non-Sense of the Whole."[7] All such evidence requires too subjective an interpretation to mean much, but it does suggest that Waldo Frank may have failed to find a significant audience because, in addition to being a literary jack-of-all-trades, he seemed to many to be a jackanapes.

Even a kind, sympathetic critic like Ernest Sutherland Bates manages to convey a dubious impression when he observes of Frank that "he writes of himself in the European manner unhampered by either reticence or bravado, with a calm and completely justified inner certainty."[8] This "inner certainty" probably indicates the major source both of Frank's failure in the United States and of his success in Latin America: his mystical concept of the nature of man is linked with his serious attempt to be a "naturalistic mystic" in his art. For despite Emerson and Whitman and writers like them who espouse and express the Great Tradition—or possibly because of them—the average American is allergic to mysticism on any level higher than that of secular Christianity or the sports pages. Hence, Frank's oracular formulation of a cosmic dimension for man encounters indifference or negativism. Munson, despite his admiration, was aware in 1923 of the damaging effect of a mystical point of view when he admitted that Frank, at the peak of his public appeal, was "projecting a free transforming religious spirit into our national literature and it is mainly this that has aroused such savage hostility against his work even within the ranks of his general faction."[9]

Frank's projection of his "naturalistic" mysticism through sexuality further confused and repulsed readers who might otherwise have responded to his plea for spiritual values—just as followers of Emerson tended to reject the blatant sexuality of his disciple Whitman. When Frank added to his symbolic treatment of sex his eloquent yet harsh attacks on pragmatism and empirical rationalism, he managed to antagonize and to alienate two widely different but potential groups of readers during the 1920's. And there is not enough change in the national psyche during the Socialistic 1930's and the Existential 1950's and 1960's to weaken the indifference to Frank's kind of thinking and writing.

The symphonic novels in which he returns to fiction in the 1930's are less individualistic and experimental than the lyric novels and are, in fact, in their social criticism close to the temper of the period; but again the "naturalistic" mysticism created a puzzling and often repelling dichotomy which at the time was also intensified by Frank's ambiguous flirtation with Communism. The modern era of best sellers begins early in the listless 1930's with a nation of unemployed readers, but Frank's new novels were overlooked as audiences turned to grubby realism in the *Studs Lonigan* trilogy, *USA*, and *The Grapes of Wrath* or to romantic escape in *Anthony Adverse* and in *Gone with the Wind*. *The Death and Birth of David Markand* and *The Bridegroom Cometh*, both substantial novels, are so completely lost in the shuffle that now even bibliographers and literary historians seldom mention them. Even contemporary critics who have to notice Frank in analyzing the literature of the 1930's and 1940's prefer to discuss his "fellow traveling" or his criticism.[10]

Perhaps the last hope for rediscovery of Waldo Frank lies in the fashionable flight-to-faith in the atomic 1960's which may alter the characteristic American insensitivity to mysticism enough to permit his simple insistence upon the cosmic dimension of man to receive a hearing without provoking either savage hostility or smug superiority. Should this minor miracle occur, it will reveal a serious writer whose work is a dynamic projection, in book after book, of an organic, total vision of life which includes and progressively integrates the personal, social, national, and esthetic single elements into a Whole—a synthesis that is now impossible in a culture devoted to linear or exclusive treatment of these elements as single. Only in cultures like those of France, Spain, and America Hispana, which have at least a tradition of totality, has there been thus far any significant or continuing interest in Waldo Frank's work. But the United States, if it is to preserve the health of its society in the long struggle with Russia and with the terror of the bomb, may need to discover an organic wholeness which will afford a stay against the confusion of fragmentation and multiplicity. Should this need arise, there are in Frank's novels and cultural studies elements of truth and of the true forms of human experience which must persist in the continuity of Western civilization if that continuity is to preserve The Great Tradition.

Writing of Don Quixote in *Virgin Spain*, Frank frames questions that could apply to his crusading: "Though he offends many and amuses more, he convinces no one. That a prophet should inspire jeers and hatred is natural: but that he should have not one disciple? And that at the end of his mission, he should recant, and call his mission folly? How can such win the love of the world?"[11] This passage would serve as an epitaph for Frank were it not for the fact that he has not jousted with windmills—and he has not recanted or accepted the folly of his mission. In a notebook entry in 1948, he answers a hypothetical critic who chides him for his egocentric refusal to accept the relative failure of his life's work:

> "*Either nothing has meaning, therefore, or I have meaning.*" Then what happens to me has meaning. This, first and last of all I must accept. . . . Necessity accepted as meaningful makes for freedom. . . . I am no sower; God is the sower; I am the sown. . . . What is my sober reply to this sceptic? "I have no measure by which to judge how a dozen of my books will impress future generations, or by which to foretell if they will be there at all . . . future generations may well belong to a culture so axially different that works like mine will be utterly worthless. . . . *But this I know*: there are elements of truth, elements of true forms

of human experience, in my books . . . which must carry over into the continuity of Western civilization, if that continuity is to be. In this sense, grains of my books will be of the spring that I shall never see, even though that spring may never name me. . . . What counts is that . . *now living* in this winter—I am seed (among others, of course) of that spring. . . . Yes: in most of my books . . . there are living seeds. . . . I cannot deny them, or me, meaning without denying meaning to the cosmos."

In *Chart for Rough Water*, Frank says of the responsibility of the writer: "To keep the values that underlie the organic sense of life and man's individual and holy share in it . . . is the function of the intellectual and artist. *His specialty is the whole.* If his work is limited to any lesser vision, embodies any smaller purpose, he is a traitor to his ancient priesthood."[12]

Frank has kept the faith. His speciality has been the whole, the recording of "proofs of God," and his books articulate the message of his ancient priesthood. "His is one of the minority voices of the twentieth century, but a minority voice not to be mistaken for a minor voice"[13]—unless contemporary man is finally ready to reject his spiritual heritage and tradition. If he is not, then Waldo Frank should be heard; for his spiritual vitality might inspire the kind of creativity which, in a dying culture, can be revolutionary.

Notes and References

Preface

1. A survey taken in 1941 of catalogues issued by Spanish language publishers lists more translations of Waldo Frank's writings than those of any other living North American writer. See Spiller and others, *Literary History of the United States* (New York, 1948), II, 1387. Van Wyck Brooks recalls that he was told "by one who was in a position to know" that Waldo Frank "was the Balzac . . . of a whole school of novelists in Argentina." See *Days of the Phoenix* (New York, 1957), p. 29.

In 1961 Aguilar published in its Biblioteca de Autores Modernos *Waldo Frank: Obras Escogidas*, a volume of 1,278 pages which reprints six of Frank's novels: *City Block, Rahab, Holiday, The Invaders, Island in the Atlantic,* and *Not Heaven.* This was followed in 1963 by a second volume, *Waldo Frank: Retratos Culturales,* which reprints *Virgin Spain, Re-discovery of America, America Hispana,* and *Birth of a World.*

2. Gorham B. Munson, *Waldo Frank: A Study* (New York, 1923), pp. 9, 60.

3. Charles I. Glicksberg, *American Literary Criticism, 1900-1950* (New York, 1951), p. 441.

4. These notebooks, which Frank started keeping in 1908 and continued throughout his career, are an invaluable record of his ideas, emotions, and projects. A kind of intellectual diary, they contain Frank's dialogues with himself while working out his beliefs in his writings. Eventually they will be placed with Frank's other papers now in the University of Pennsylvania Library. All quotations from Frank in this Preface are from these notebooks.

Chapter One

1. *Our America* (New York, 1919), pp. 231-32.

2. Biographical and bibliographical details in this chapter are taken from William Bittner, *The Novels of Waldo Frank* (Philadelphia, 1958), pp. 20-32; all subsequent quotations unless otherwise indicated are from Frank's *In the American Jungle* (New York, 1937), pp. 3-15. Double sets of quotation marks have been dispensed with in nearly all cases throughout this text.

Chapter Two

1. *The Unwelcome Man* (Boston, 1917), p. xi. All subsequent quotations in this section are from the novel unless otherwise identified.

2. Frederick J. Hoffman, *Freudianism and the Literary Mind* (New York, 1959), pp. 257-63.

3. Bittner, p. 16.

4. Brooks, p. 17.

5. *Salvos* (New York, 1924), pp. 31-32.
6. *Re-discovery of America* (New York, 1929), p. 318.
7. Typescript with the title *Memoir of Waldo Frank*, p. 134. A first draft of Parts I and II of this manuscript, covering the years to 1937, is among the Frank papers in the University of Pennsylvania Library.
8. *Salvos*, p. 121. The other quotations in this paragraph are from this volume of essays also, which includes *The Art of the Vieux Colombier*.
9. *Our America*, p. ix, "Foreword" to the American Edition. All subsequent quotations in the next section are from this work unless otherwise identified.
10. "Herald of the Twenties," (University of Houston) *Forum*, III (Fall, 1961), 11-14.
11. Jerome W. Kloucek, *Waldo Frank: The Ground of His Mind and Art* (Ann Arbor, 1963), p. 433.
12. *Ibid.*, p. 434. Frank writes that "the Kansas episode with the Non-Partisan League is almost literally transposed into the Western chapters of *The Death and Birth of David Markand.*" *Memoir*, p. 163.
13. All subsequent quotations in this section are from *The Dark Mother* unless otherwise indicated.
14. Munson, *Waldo Frank: A Study*, p. 31.
15. *Ibid.*, p. 34.
16. Bittner, p. 48.
17. In a footnote in *Memoir*, p. 168, Frank observes that "Like *The Unwelcome Man*," *The Dark Mother* "is an experiment that failed, because no technique had been developed to express the book's specific form of vision."

Chapter Three

1. Bittner, p. 77.
2. Although published before *City Block* (Darien, 1922), *Rahab* (New York, 1922) grew out of a theme for a short story sketched for *City Block*. Bittner, p. 76. Frank recalled that both books encountered difficulties with censorship because of the rampant "Comstockery of the 1920's." The printers in New England refused to set *Rahab*, charging that it was "obscene and sacrilegious." *Memoir*, p. 176.
3. Bittner, p. 61.
4. *Memoir*, p. 168.
5. *Ibid.*, pp. 167-68.
6. This and all subsequent quotations in this section are from *Rahab* unless otherwise indicated.
7. Kloucek reads the novel in terms of the mystic's characteristic experience of awakening, purification, illumination. Fanny's reliving of her sad life, coupled with her attempt to think, "creates the psychic state for Fanny's full mystic illumination . . . . she finds humility, learns to accept and to love life and the world as it is without questioning or judging it, so that she at last comes to see that even the men and women who frequent her house of prostitution, '. . . held a grain of loveliness'; and in the end this thinking graduates into the state of contemplation leading to mystic illumination." Kloucek, pp. 492-93.
8. All quotations in this paragraph are from Frank's description of his own mystical experience, which is recorded in Notebook VII under the title *Sights*.

9. The first version of "The Altar of the World" was written in March, 1916; "Candles" appeared as "The Candles of Romance" in *Smart Set*, February, 1917; "The Table" appeared as "Rudd" in *Seven Arts*, August, 1917. Frank thought that "The Table" was the most satisfactory of all his stories. *Memoir*, p. 168.

10. This and all subsequent quotations in this section are from *City Block* unless otherwise identified.

11. Bittner, p. 71.

12. Kloucek, p. 495.

13. Frank remembered how George W. Carver solved an awkward situation at the supper following the speech. Two tables had been placed in a screened-off area of the gymnasium: one was set for a dozen or more faculty members; the other, two yards away, had places for Frank and his wife. When Frank protested the arrangement and the Director of Tuskegee refused to break "the iron custom of the South" for fear of "dire consequences," George Carver, "whose grizzled face of an angel revealed why he was loved," picked up his plate and stood while he ate, thereby "converting the dinner into an integrated buffet." *Memoir*, p. 171.

14. This and all subsequent quotations in this section are from *Holiday* unless otherwise identified.

15. Kloucek, p. 496, quoting from "Black Men and White," *Brentano's Book Chat*, II (Thanksgiving, 1923), 25-26.

16. Frank's interest in unanimism began with his discovery of Jules Romains in 1916, whose book of poems, *La Vie Unanime* (1908), gave the movement its name. The most significant and influential theory of unanimism for Frank was that the group is of first importance; and the individual, especially the writer, can gain power and meaning only by merging with the group. See Kloucek, pp. 370-78, for a detailed discussion of the philosophic, social, and esthetic aspects of unanimism. See also Frank's essay "A Prophet in France," *Salvos*, pp. 77-91.

17. Bittner, p. 104. "Joyce was what the new jargon becoming current called an introvert but because it was absolute his introversion was not schizoid; it was a whole world of its own, creating as mankind had, from its mysterious past its own language. Joyce, it seemed to Frank, resembled the bottle of white wine before him. He was slender, gracefully; he was cold, externally; like the wine he had an inner glow blended into a dry and dominant savor. He was thin and spare-shouldered like a student, trim-bearded like a pedagogue, and his pale eyes looked inward with a compassion for his fellows that was both hot and distant.

"Later, when Waldo knew his family: his wife, his son and his son's wife, he recognized the patriarchal grasp of the man on those for whom he felt affection. And this embraced his friends." *Memoir*, p. 200.

18. Subsequent quotations in this section come from various essays in this collection.

19. All subsequent quotations in this section are from *Chalk Face* unless otherwise indicated.

20. Kloucek, p. 499.

21. Quoted in Bittner, p. 105.

22. Harlan Hatcher, *Creating the Modern American Novel* (New York, 1935), p. 178.

Chapter Four

1. This and all subsequent quotations in this section are from *Virgin Spain*—the first edition—unless otherwise identified.
2. M. J. Benardete (ed.), *Waldo Frank in America Hispana* (New York, 1930), pp. 246-47. This volume was compiled from the articles and laudatory addresses inspired among Latin Americans by Frank's tour.
3. Kloucek, p. 270. See also pp. 510-13 for details of the critical reception of *Virgin Spain*.
4. *Memoir*, p. 219.

Chapter Five

1. This and all subsequent quotations in this section come from various essays in the collection.
2. All subsequent quotations in this section are from *The Re-discovery of America* unless otherwise indicated.
3. All subsequent quotations in this section are from *America Hispana* unless otherwise indicated.
4. Kloucek, p. 522.
5. "Waldo Frank in the Hispanic World: The First Phase," *Hispania*, XLIV (December, 1961), 632. "As a literary ambassador to Latin America Waldo was unique, for there could scarcely ever have been another North American who was able to enter that world by his deep inner line. . . . He brought his own countrymen their first news of the vivid intellectual life of the South . . ." Brooks, p. 29.
6. ". . . the only serious North American author who exercised a direct influence in America Hispana during the twenties was Waldo Frank." Spiller and others, *Literary History of the United States*, p. 1387.

Chapter Six

1. All subsequent quotations in the next section are from *Dawn in Russia* unless otherwise indicated.
2. Kloucek, p. 442 (footnote), quoting an English translation of a Spanish text. Most of the details regarding Frank's political activities during this period of his career are drawn from Kloucek, pp. 441ff.
3. *Memoir*, p. 278.
4. "Where I Stand and How I Got There," *New Masses*, VIII (September, 1932), 7.
5. Kloucek, p. 527.
6. Bittner, pp. 132, 134.
7. This and all subsequent quotations in this section are from *The Death and Birth of David Markand* unless otherwise identified.
8. Kloucek, p. 527.

Chapter Seven

1. This and all subsequent quotations in this section come from various essays in the collection.
2. *Memoir*, p. 284.
3. *Ibid.*, p. 286.
4. This and all subsequent quotations in this section are from *The Bridegroom Cometh* unless otherwise identified.

5. Kloucek, p. 529.
6. Bittner, p. 161.

Chapter Eight

1. Bittner, pp. 167-68.
2. This and all subsequent quotations in this section are from *Chart for Rough Water* unless otherwise identified.
3. This and all subsequent quotations in this section are from *Summer Never Ends* unless otherwise identified.
4. Bittner, pp. 172-73.
5. This and all subsequent quotations in this section are from *South American Journey* unless otherwise identified.
6. The quotations in this and the following paragraph come from the collection.

Chapter Nine

1. This and all subsequent quotations in this section are from *Island in the Atlantic* unless otherwise identified.
2. Bittner, p. 191.
3. This and all subsequent quotations in this section are from *The Invaders* unless otherwise identified.

Chapter Ten

1. This and all subsequent quotations in this section are from *The Birth of a World* unless otherwise identified.
2. This and all subsequent quotations in this section are from *Not Heaven* unless otherwise identified.
3. This and all subsequent quotations in this section are from *Bridgehead: The Drama of Israel* unless otherwise identified.
4. Bittner, p. 213.

Chapter Eleven

1. All subsequent quotations in this section are from *The Rediscovery of Man* unless otherwise identified.
2. This and all subsequent quotations in this section are from *Cuba: Prophetic Island* unless otherwise identified.

Chapter Twelve

1. Munson, *Waldo Frank: A Study*, pp. 9, 60.
2. See Joseph W. Beach, *The Twentieth Century Novel* (New York, 1932), p. 497: "I find myself incapable of evaluating the work of Waldo Frank in the whole. I do not know whether it is sound, whether it has a significance on which one can rest as on something solid." See also Brooks, pp. 25-26: "But, greatly liking some of his novels,—and the humanity of them all,—I was always more at home with his non-fictional writing. . . . It seemed to me that . . . he was rather an intellectual than a novelist proper. . . ."
3. Something of the relative status of Frank and Lewis in 1921 is suggested by the difference in critical attention accorded their novels. For example, *The Dial* (January, 1921) gives a half dozen pages to an essay

review of *The Unwelcome Man* and *The Dark Mother*; *Main Street* receives a paragraph notation: ". . . a Young Wives Tale of Minnesota. . . . The book has more social than artistic implications" (p. 106).

4. See Kloucek, p. 511.
5. Lewis Gannett, "Books and Things," New York *Herald Tribune*, May 20, 1943.
6. *The Dial*, LXX (January, 1921), 100, 103.
7. *The Modern Quarterly*, V (Winter, 1930-31), 509-10: "His mysticism is too diffuse to be a principle of organization, his lyricism is too personal to stir a group into consciousness of common destiny, and his thinking too inchoate to clearly formulate the problems at issue."
8. New York *Herald Tribune Books*, April 18, 1937, p. 7.
9. Munson, *Waldo Frank: A Study*, p. 61.
10. See Daniel Aaron, *Writers on the Left: Episodes in American Literary Communism* (New York, 1961), *passim*, and Glicksberg, *op. cit.*, pp. 439 ff. *Literary History of the United States* has seven entries for Frank, but only one mentions a novel (*City Block*), an example of his "massive social studies" (p. 1235), commenting only on his influence in America Hispana (p. 1387). Arthur H. Quinn (ed.), *The Literature of the American People*, (New York, 1951), p. 956, cites only *The Re-discovery of America*, a book which contributed to the movement of critics toward "the Marxist position."
11. *Virgin Spain*, p. 214.
12. *Chart for Rough Water*, p. 46.
13. Kloucek, p. 537.

Selected Bibliography

I PRIMARY SOURCES

A Note on Manuscript Sources and Bibliography

Personal notebooks, letters received by Frank, and manuscripts of published and unpublished material are now owned by the University of Pennsylvania and are deposited in its Rare Book and Manuscript Collection.

The following bibliography represents only a selection of the published major items. For a much more inclusive listing see Jerome W. Kloucek, *Waldo Frank: The Ground of His Mind and Art* (Ann Arbor, Michigan: University Microfilms, Inc., 1963), pp. 544-73, which records over two hundred contributions by Frank to periodicals and other publications. Kloucek has also compiled an extensive typescript of all published work by and about Frank, including all of the reprints in Latin American journals.

1. *Published Novels*

The Unwelcome Man: A Novel. Boston: Little Brown and Company, 1917.
The Dark Mother: A Novel. New York: Boni and Liveright, 1920.
Rahab. New York: Boni and Liveright, 1922.
City Block. Darien, Connecticut: By the author, 1922; reissued, New York: Charles Scribner's Sons, 1932.
Holiday. New York: Boni and Liveright, 1923.
Chalk Face. New York: Boni and Liveright, 1924.
The Death and Birth of David Markand: An American Story. New York and London: Charles Scribner's Sons, 1934.
The Bridegroom Cometh. London: Gollancz, 1938; New York: Doubleday, Doran and Company, 1939.
Summer Never Ends: A Modern Love Story. New York: Duell, Sloan and Pearce, 1941.
Island in the Atlantic: A Novel. New York: Duell, Sloan and Pearce, 1946.
The Invaders: A Novel. New York: Duell, Sloan and Pearce, 1948.
Not Heaven: A Novel in the Form of Prelude, Variations, and Theme. New York: Hermitage House, 1953.

2. *Cultural History and Criticism*

Our America. New York: Boni and Liveright, 1919; London edition in 1922 with the title *The New American.*
Virgin Spain: Scenes from the Spiritual Drama of a Great People. New York: Boni and Liveright, 1926; revised edition, New York: Duell, Sloan and Pearce, 1942.
The Re-discovery of America: An Introduction to a Philosophy of American Life. New York and London: Charles Scribner's Sons, 1929.
America Hispana: A Portrait and a Prospect. New York and London: Charles Scribner's Sons, 1931; reissued with the title *America Hispana: South of Us; the Characters of the Countries and the People of Central and South America.* New York: Garden City, 1940.
Dawn in Russia: The Record of a Journey. New York and London: Charles Scribner's Sons, 1932.
In the American Jungle (1925-1936). New York: Farrar & Rinehart, 1937.

Chart for Rough Water: Our Role in a New World. New York: Doubleday, Doran and Company, 1940.
South American Journey. New York: Duell, Sloan and Pearce, 1943.
The Jew in Our Day. New York: Duell, Sloan and Pearce, 1944.
Birth of a World: Bolivar in Terms of His Peoples. Boston: Houghton Mifflin Company, 1951.
Bridgehead: The Drama of Israel. New York: George Braziller, 1957.
The Rediscovery of Man: A Memoir and a Methodology of Modern Life. New York: George Braziller, 1958.
Cuba: Prophetic Island. New York: Marzani and Munsell, 1961.

3. *Literary Criticism*

The Art of the Vieux Colombier: A Contribution of France to the Contemporary Stage. Paris and New York: Editions de la Nouvelle Revue Française, 1918; reprinted in *Salvos*, pp. 119-67.
Salvos: An Informal Book about Books and Plays. New York: Boni and Liveright, 1924.
Time Exposures: By Search-Light. New York: Boni and Liveright, 1926; published anonymously.

4. *Plays*

New Year's Eve: A Play. New York and London: Charles Scribner's Sons, 1929.

5. *Lectures Published Only in Spanish*

Primer mensaje a la América Hispana. Madrid: Revista de Occidente, 1930.
Ustedes y Nosotros: Nuevo Mesaje a Ibero-America. Buenos Aires: Editorial Losada, 1942.

SECONDARY SOURCES

Kloucek lists over a hundred entries containing criticisms and comments about Waldo Frank. The following list represents only a sampling of the more important ones.

AARON, DANIEL. *Writers on the Left: Episodes in American Literary Communism.* New York: Harcourt, Brace and World, 1961. Analyzes the reaction of American writers to the "idea of communism" from 1912 to 1940.
BATES, ERNEST SUTHERLAND. "Waldo Frank, Still Discovering America," New York *Herald Tribune Books*, April 18, 1937, p. 7. Review of *In the American Jungle.*
BEACH, JOSEPH W. *The Twentieth Century Novel.* New York and London: D. Appleton-Century Company, 1932. Analysis of *City Block* and Frank's "Expressionism."
BENARDETE, M. J. (ed.). *Waldo Frank in America Hispana.* New York: Instituto de las Espana, 1930. Laudatory articles and speeches by Latin Americans inspired by Frank's first lecture tour in South America.
BITTNER, WILLIAM. *The Novels of Waldo Frank.* Philadelphia: University of Pennsylvania Press, 1958. The best and only detailed discussion of all of the novels.
———. "Waldo Frank as Novelist," *Literary Review*, I (Summer, 1958), 478-84.

BROOKS, VAN WYCK. *Days of the Phoenix.* New York: E. P. Dutton and Company, 1957. Sketches of writers whom the author knew in the 1920's and with whom he was associated on the *Seven Arts,* the *Freeman,* and the *Dial.*

CHAPMAN, ARNOLD. "Waldo Frank in the Hispanic World: The First Phase," *Hispania,* XLIV (December, 1961), 626-34.

———. "Waldo Frank in Spanish America: Between Journeys, 1924-1929," *Hispania,* XLVII (September, 1964), 510-21.

GANNETT, LEWIS. "Books and Things," New York *Herald Tribune,* May 20, 1943. Review of *America Hispana.*

GLICKSBERG, CHARLES I., (ed.). "Waldo Frank," *American Literary Criticism.* New York: Hendricks House, 1951. Pages 439-41.

———. "Waldo Frank: Critic of America," *South Atlantic Quarterly,* XXXV (January, 1936), 13-26. Favorable survey of Frank's social criticism of America.

HATCHER, HARLAN. *Creating the Modern American Novel.* New York: Farrar and Rinehart, 1935. Favorable commentary on the "impressionistic" techniques in the "lyric novels" and in *The Death and Birth of David Markand.*

HEMINGWAY, ERNEST. *Death in the Afternoon.* New York and London: Charles Scribner's Sons, 1932. Attack upon Waldo Frank and his view of Spain.

HOFFMAN, FREDERICK J. *Freudianism and the Literary Mind.* New York: Grove Press, 1959. A brief but helpful analysis of Frank's criticism and fiction.

KLOUCEK, JEROME W. *Waldo Frank: The Ground of His Mind and Art.* Ann Arbor, Michigan: University Microfilms, Inc., 1963. Brilliant, scholarly study of the sources and tenets of Frank's philosophy, psychology, religion, and art.

MUNSON, GORHAM. "Herald of the Twenties," (University of Houston) *Forum,* III (Fall, 1961), 4-14.

———. "Prose for Fiction: Waldo Frank," *Style and Form in American Prose.* Garden City: Doubleday, Doran and Company, 1929. Analyzes some of the narrative techniques in the novels.

———. *Waldo Frank: A Study.* New York: Boni and Liveright, 1923. This early favorable commentary on Frank's first novels is remarkably perceptive for its time.

O'BRIEN, EDWARD J. *The Advance of the American Short Story.* New York: Dodd, Mead and Company, 1923. Reflects the early favorable evaluation of Frank's stories.

READ, HERBERT. "The Attributes of Criticism," *Reason and Romanticism.* London: Faber and Gwyer, 1926.

ROSENFELD, PAUL. *Men Seen.* New York: The Dial Press, 1925. Revised, expanded version of critical review of the early novels in "Novels of Waldo Frank," *Dial,* LXX (January, 1921), 95-105.

Waldo Frank: Obras Escogidas. Mexico: Aguilar, 1961. (Páginas 9-37: prólogo de Ramón Barce.)

Waldo Frank: Retratos Culturales. Mexico: Aguilar, 1963. (Páginas 9-35: prólogo de Antonio Espina con 68 illustraciones.)

WILLINGHAM, JOHN R. "The Achievement of Waldo Frank," *Literary Review,* I (Summer, 1958), 465-77.

Index